gateway science

HIGHER

revision guide

OCR
Additional
Science

for GCSE

Elaine Gill • Roger Norris • Carol Tear

Series editor: Bob McDuell

Heinemann

Heinemann is an imprint of Pearson Education Limited, a company incorporated in England and Wales, having its registered office at Edinburgh Gate, Harlow, Essex, CM20 2JE. Registered company number: 872828

Heinemann is a registered trademark of Pearson Education Limited

© Harcourt Education Limited 2007

First published 2007

11
10 9 8 7 6 5 4

British Library Cataloguing in Publication Data is available from the British Library on request.

ISBN: 978 0 435675 46 2

Designed by Wooden Ark
Project managed, edited and typeset by Bookcraft Ltd (Alex Sharpe, Project Manager)

Pearson project team: David Cooke, Andrew Halcro-Johnston, Ross Laman, Sarah Ross, Ruth Simms, Iti Singh, Peter Stratton

Original illustrations © Harcourt Education Limited 2007

Illustrated by Bookcraft India Pvt Ltd (Gemma Raj), HL Studios

Printed in China (CTPS/04)

Cover photo © Getty Images

Every effort has been made to contact copyright holders of material reproduced in this book. Any omissions will be rectified in subsequent printings if notice is given to the publishers.

About this book

This OCR Gateway Additional Science revision guide will help you revise for the OCR Gateway higher exams. One exam consists of modules B3, C3 and P3 and the other of B4, C4 and P4. The guide summarises what you have learnt and links directly to the OCR Additional Science specification.

This guide is broken down into the six modules: B3, B4, C3, C4, P3 and P4. Each module covers eight items (a–h), for example B3a–B3h. You will find some items are combined into one section, for example B3d & B3e.

Each section starts with a **learning outcome** which summarises the main points covered. This will help you to focus on what you need to revise in that section.

Key words are shown in bold and you will find them indexed at the back of the guide. **Equations** are highlighted to help you use and apply them.

The exam may ask you to consider ideas about 'How science works'. The **How science works** boxes will help you apply this thinking to your answers. Remember that you should be continually questioning how scientists collect data, use and interpret evidence.

Exam tips highlight common mistakes and give you advice about exam preparation so you can achieve better grades.

You will find lots of simple, full colour diagrams, including **spider diagrams**, to help with your revision and to make the content more digestible. Try drawing your own spider diagrams to help you remember key concepts.

We have given you **'Test yourself' questions** at the end of each section to help you to check that you have understood the content. Use the **answers** at the back of the guide to check whether you have got them all correct – if not, go back and revise that section again.

The revision guide is based on the new specification and the example **exam-style questions** on page 74 will give you valuable preparation for the exams.

Remember that these questions are for revision and homework. The exams will also contain some recall and one-mark questions. In your revision you should think beyond the basic ideas so that you have a better understanding for the exams.

The **answers** that follow the questions will allow you to check your progress and improve next time.

Good luck with your exams!

Contents

B3a Molecules of life

After revising this item you should:

- be able to explain that respiration takes place in mitochondria of cells, understand the structure of DNA and its role in the production of proteins and understand how enzymes work.

Mitochondria

Organisms are made up of cells. Cells are very small and can only be seen using a microscope. Microscopes have been improved and we can see more and more detail.

Using an electron microscope, we can see the **mitochondria**.

These are the site of respiration.

Respiration provides energy for all life processes.

Mitochondria contain enzymes that carry out the final stages of respiration.

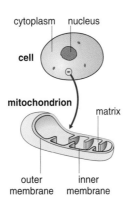

Proteins

Proteins are made up of chains of amino acids. The amino acids each cell uses come from the protein in our diet.

Some foods do not contain all the amino acids we need. The liver can change some amino acids into others (transamination). But essential amino acids must be obtained from our food.

Each protein has its own number and sequence of amino acids. This results in different shaped molecules which have different functions. For example:

- enzymes are folded into a compact 3D shape
- structural proteins are longer and often wound into a triple helix to give more strength.

The cell's nucleus controls which proteins the cell makes (protein synthesis). The instructions for this are carried in the code of DNA bases in the nucleus.

DNA

Chromosomes in the nucleus are made of DNA. DNA is made of two strands of organic bases twisted into a spiral. This is called a **double helix**.

Between the two strands are cross-links formed by two of the bases.

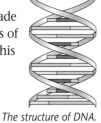

The structure of DNA.

There are four bases altogether: A, T, C and G. They pair up in a specific way, which we call **complementary base pairing**.

The diagrams show the structure of DNA and how the bases are arranged.

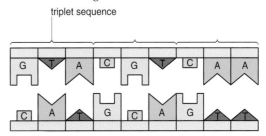

Strand of DNA showing detail of bases.

The order of bases codes for the order of amino acids in a protein.

- Each amino acid is coded by a sequence of three bases called the triplet code.
- The total sequence of bases that codes for a protein is a gene.
- The number of triplets in one gene varies.

The DNA can copy itself (DNA replication) and does this before a cell divides.

1. The two strands 'unzip' to form single strands.
2. New bases join up with the exposed bases by complementary base pairing.
3. Two complete double strands are formed.

Each new strand is identical to the original.

After **fertilisation** there is one fertilised egg cell. The DNA in the nucleus of this cell copies itself and the cell divides into two. Each new cell has identical DNA. This process continues until there are millions of cells in an adult.

DNA fingerprints

The DNA of each person is unique and can be used to identify a person. To do this a DNA fingerprint must be made.

The stages in making a DNA fingerprint are:
1 Isolate DNA from cells.
2 Fragment DNA.
3 Separate the DNA fragments by electrophoresis.
4 Compare with a reference sample.

This process is shown in the next diagram.

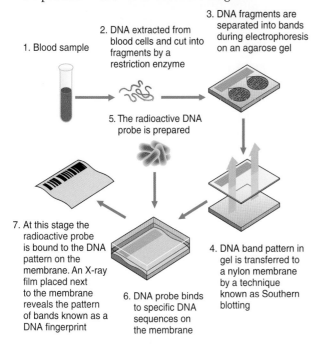

1. Blood sample

2. DNA extracted from blood cells and cut into fragments by a restriction enzyme

3. DNA fragments are separated into bands during electrophoresis on an agarose gel

5. The radioactive DNA probe is prepared

7. At this stage the radioactive probe is bound to the DNA pattern on the membrane. An X-ray film placed next to the membrane reveals the pattern of bands known as a DNA fingerprint

6. DNA probe binds to specific DNA sequences on the membrane

4. DNA band pattern in gel is transferred to a nylon membrane by a technique known as Southern blotting

How science works

Forensic scientists use DNA fingerprinting to:
- confirm a suspect was at a crime scene
- confirm a suspect was not at a crime scene
- prove or disprove a parent of a child.

Enzymes

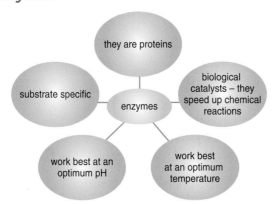

they are proteins

substrate specific

enzymes

biological catalysts – they speed up chemical reactions

work best at an optimum pH

work best at an optimum temperature

Each enzyme catalyses one reaction only. It is highly specific to a single substrate.

Each protein has its own number and sequence of amino acids. This results in different shaped enzyme molecules which have different functions.

The specificity of an enzyme is explained by the way it works.
- The chemical it reacts with is the **substrate**.
- The substrate fits into the **active site** of the enzyme.
- The shape of the active site means that only a substrate that has a complementary shape can fit into it – similar to a lock and key.

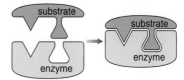

substrate

enzyme

substrate

enzyme

Optimum temperature and pH

An enzyme works best at one, optimum temperature.
- Below this temperature the rate of reaction is slower, but the enzyme still works if the temperature rises again.
- Above this temperature the rate slows down and stops.

An enzyme works best at one pH. Above or below the optimum pH the structure of the enzyme is changed.

High temperatures and extremes of pH will change the shape of the enzyme's active site. Once changed, it cannot regain the correct shape and so the enzyme cannot catalyse reactions. It is said to be **denatured**.

The following graphs show the effect of changing temperature and pH on the rate of an enzyme-controlled reaction.

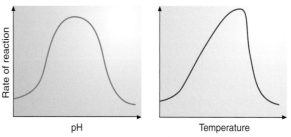

Rate of reaction

pH

Temperature

Most enzymes work best at body temperature (37°C) and at a specific pH, which is different for each enzyme.

Test yourself

1. The table shows the sequence of three bases for four amino acids.

Sequence of three bases	Amino acid
CGT	P
CAA	Q
CAG	R
GTA	S

Look at the strand of DNA showing the base sequence (page 2).

  (a) Give the order of amino acids that the bases in the upper strand code for.
  (b) If the last base A was changed to G, would the amino acids be different? If so, how would they be different?

2. Describe complementary base pairing.

3. Name three chemical reactions in a living cell that are catalysed by enzymes.

4. Mary washed the football team's shirts after a match. They had lots of grass stains on them. She used a biological washing powder and washed the shirts at 100°C but the stains did not come out. Explain why.

5. The DNA fingerprints shown are those of a mother, child and possible father.

  (a) Is this the father of the child?
  (b) Explain your answer.

B3b Diffusion

After revising this item you should:

- be able to explain how materials move through living organisms by diffusion, understand where diffusion occurs in animal and plant cells and explain the importance of diffusion in these cells.

Moving particles

Inside our bodies substances move in and out of cells by diffusion through the cell membrane.

Diffusion is:

- the movement of a substance from an area of its high concentration to an area of its low concentration along a **concentration gradient**.

It is the net movement of particles.

- Particles move from high to low concentration and from low to high concentration but overall more move from high to low.
- Each particle is constantly moving at random and tends to spread out.

The diagram shows the useful substances a cell gains and the waste products it gets rid of by diffusion.

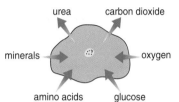

The rate of diffusion is increased by:

- a shorter diffusion distance
- a greater difference in concentration (gradient)
- a larger surface area.

Diffusion in animals

The following table gives some examples of diffusion in animals.

Where diffusion occurs	What diffuses	From where	To where
small intestine	digested food	**lumen** of small intestine	blood
lungs	oxygen	air in **alveoli**	blood
lungs	carbon dioxide	blood	air in alveoli
placenta	digested food and oxygen	mother's blood	fetal blood
placenta	carbon dioxide and waste	fetal blood	mother's blood
synapse	chemical **transmitter substances**	end of a neurone	beginning of another neurone

Each body part is adapted as follows:

1 Alveoli in lungs for efficient gaseous exchange.
- **Permeable**.   • Moist.
- Large surface area.   • Good blood supply.
- Alveoli wall one cell thick.

Exam tip

Avoid the mistake of saying 'cell wall is one cell thick' – remember that animal cells do not have cell walls, only cell membranes.

2 Small intestine for food absorption.
- Long.
- Large surface area (**villi** and **microvilli**).
- Permeable surface.
- Good blood supply.

3 Placenta to increase the rate of diffusion to the **fetus**.
- Large surface area.   • Villi.
- Good blood supply.

4 The synapse, which transmitter substances diffuse across to carry signals from one neurone to the next.
- Transmitter substances are only produced on one side of the synapse.
- They are in high concentration on one side and low concentration on the other.
- The gap is tiny.

Diffusion in plants

The following table gives some examples of diffusion in plants.

Where diffusion occurs	What diffuses	From where	To where
leaves	oxygen and carbon dioxide	stomata/air	air/stomata
leaves	water vapour	leaf (intercellular spaces)	air

The leaves are adapted to increase the rate of carbon dioxide and oxygen diffusion:
- They have **stomata** on their bottom surface.
- They are flat and thin to give a large surface area.
- There are air spaces inside the leaves.

Plants use oxygen and produce carbon dioxide during respiration, which takes place in all plant cells both day and night. In addition they use carbon dioxide and produce oxygen during photosynthesis during the day.

Test yourself

1 Describe one way in which the surface area of a cell can be increased.

2 What are villi and microvilli? What part do they play in absorption?

3 List the features that all diffusion surfaces have in common.

4 During which part of the day does diffusion take place in plants?

5 Natasha used some perfume at the back of the laboratory. Students sitting near her complained about the smell but the teacher at the front ignored them – she could smell nothing. Explain why the students could smell the perfume but the teacher could not.

B3c Keep it moving

After revising this item you should:

- be able to explain how parts of the blood are adapted for their function, understand how the circulatory system works and explain the problems of replacing hearts with transplants and artificial parts.

Blood

The blood is made up of:
- **red blood cells**
- **white blood cells**
- **plasma**.

Red blood cells are well adapted to carry out their function.

Red blood cell adaptation	How this helps with its function
small size	can fit through narrow blood vessels
bi-concave disc shape	gives a large surface area to volume ratio to gain or lose oxygen more quickly
no nucleus	more **haemoglobin** can fit in the cell
contains haemoglobin	combines with oxygen to form **oxyhaemoglobin** in the lungs, and gives up the oxygen in the tissues

White blood cells:

- are bigger than red blood cells
- have a flexible shape to engulf disease organisms.

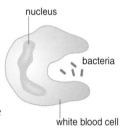

Plasma is the liquid part of the blood which carries cells and substances around the body.

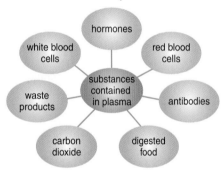

Circulatory system

The circulatory system consists of the heart and the blood vessels.

The parts work together to transport substances around the body.

- **Arteries** transport blood away from the heart.
- **Veins** transport blood to the heart.
- **Capillaries** are involved in exchange of substances in the tissues.

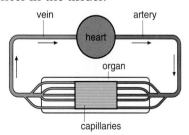

The following table shows how blood vessels are adapted for their role in carrying blood to and from the heart.

Arteries	Veins	Capillaries
thick, muscular and elastic wall – withstands high pressure	<ul><li>large lumen – eases blood flow</li><li>valves – prevent backflow of blood</li></ul>	walls are one cell thick and permeable – allows for rapid diffusion of glucose and oxygen to the tissues and carbon dioxide and waste from the tissues

The heart

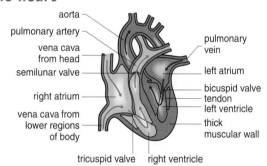

The following table shows the functions of the main parts of the heart.

Part	Function
right **atrium**	to receive blood from the body and pass it to the right ventricle
left atrium	to receive blood from the lungs and pass it to the left ventricle
right **ventricle**	to receive blood from the right atrium and pump it to the lungs
left ventricle	to receive blood from the left atrium and to pump it to the body
valves – **semilunar**, **bicuspid, tricuspid**	to stop blood flowing backwards
four blood vessels – **vena cava, pulmonary artery**, pulmonary vein, **aorta**	to take blood into or out of the heart

The left ventricle wall is thicker than the right ventricle wall because it pumps blood all round the body – the right ventricle only pumps blood as far as the lungs.

Exam tip

You need to know where each structure is and what it does. Try adding labels in the correct places to an unlabelled diagram of the heart.

Remember also that:

- **v**ena cava is a **v**ein, **a**orta is an **a**rtery
- *chambers of the heart contract to push blood*
- *valves stop backflow of blood.*

Mammals have a **double circulatory** system. Blood has to pass through the heart twice on each full circuit of the body.

This means that higher pressures can be established so more blood flows to the tissues.

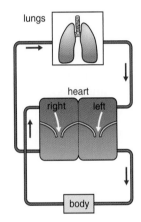

Cholesterol

The amount of **cholesterol** in the arteries is linked to how much cholesterol is in the food you eat.

Cholesterol builds up in the arteries to form a **plaque**, which can restrict blood flow or cause a blockage.

Heart problems

If the blockage is in an artery supplying the heart muscle (coronary artery), then part of the heart is starved of oxygen and dies. This can cause a heart attack.

This can be remedied by a heart transplant. However, there can be many problems with the supply of donor hearts for transplant:

- There is a shortage of donor hearts.
- Tissues must match.
- Blood groups must be the same.
- The size should be the same.
- The age of donor and recipient should be the same.

There is also the risk that the recipient's body will reject the donor heart. Heart patients have to take anti-rejection drugs and other drugs for the rest of their life.

Mechanical replacements, such as artificial pacemakers and valves, can be used instead. But these can have other problems:

- Unsuitable size of parts.
- A power supply is needed.
- The body may react to the artificial parts.

The following table summarises the advantages and disadvantages of artificial pacemakers and valves compared with transplants.

Advantages	Disadvantages
readily available – no wait for suitable donor heart no need for anti-rejection drugs	pacemaker needs a battery which must be replaced regularly mechanical valves can go wrong difficult to get parts in the right sizes materials can cause allergic reactions harder for a pacemaker to change its rate during exercise than a transplant heart

Test yourself

1 Where does the pulmonary artery carry blood from and to?

2 The diagram shows sections through two arteries A and B.

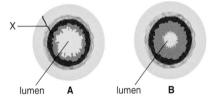

   (a) Which artery shows a build up of cholesterol? How does cholesterol affect the circulation?
   (b) What does X represent? How would X be different in a vein?

3 Explain how a red blood cell is adapted to carry oxygen around the body.

4 A fish has a single circulation. Its blood passes through the heart to the gills, then to the body and back to the heart. How is the double circulation of a human different to this?

5 Why is a heart transplant better than a pacemaker if the patient wants to do a lot of exercise?

B3d Divide and rule & B3e Growing up

Cell division

Cells can divide in one of two ways:

- **Mitosis** – allows growth and specialisation of cells in an organism.
- **Meiosis** – produces **gametes** (eggs and sperm) during sexual reproduction.

Mitosis allows organisms to grow by increasing the number of cells. It leads to **multicellular** organisms. The advantages of being multicellular are shown in the following spider diagram.

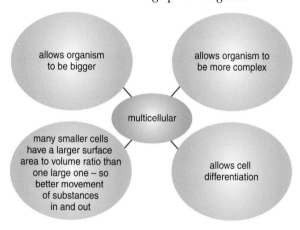

Mitosis

In mammals, body cells are **diploid** (they have two of each chromosome). Human body cells contain 46 chromosomes in 23 pairs.

During mitosis:

- the chromosomes are copied
- the copies divide and move to opposite poles of the cell
- each new cell is genetically identical to the original one.

1 a cell has four chromosomes, two pairs

2 chromosomes are copied

3 chromosomes from one line down the centre of the cell

4 one copy of each chromosome moves to the opposite pole of the cell

Mitosis.

Meiosis

Meiosis produces gametes (sex cells). It occurs only in the sex organs.

Gametes are **haploid** – they contain one of each chromosome. Gametes join at fertilisation to produce a diploid **zygote**.

As any sperm can fertilise any egg, the possible combinations of chromosomes is endless. This produces variation.

During meiosis:

- chromosomes are copied and the copies stay together
- the pairs of chromosomes then separate and move to opposite poles of the cell
- the cell divides to form two cells
- each chromosome copy divides to opposite poles of the cell
- the two cells divide again
- the number of chromosomes is halved in each new cell.

1 a cell has four chromosomes, two pairs

2 chromosome are copied

3 chromosome pairs line up side by side

4 the copies split to produce four cells, each containing half the original number of chromosomes

Meiosis.

The following diagram shows that a sperm cell is adapted to its function.

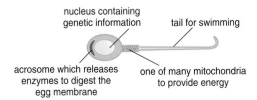

Growing up

All plants and animals are made of one or more cells.

Animal cells contain:
- nucleus
- membrane
- cytoplasm

Plant cells contain:
- nucleus
- membrane
- cytoplasm
- chloroplasts
- cell wall
- large vacuole

The following table shows the difference in growth of animals and plants.

Animals	Plants
grow to a finite size	grow continuously
cells stop growing at a certain size	greater enlargement of cells means they can grow to greater heights
cell division happens over the whole body	cell division happens at tips of roots and shoots
lose ability to **differentiate** at an early stage	retain the ability to differentiate

Some cells produced by mitosis are undifferentiated. Undifferentiated cells are called **stem cells**. These cells can develop into different cells tissues and organs. Examples in animals are muscle and blood cells.

How science works

Scientific research shows that stem cells can be used to grow different types of cells in the laboratory. These cells could be used to provide replacement parts for human organs that no longer function. The stem cells usually come from an embryo.

Write down one argument supporting stem cell research and one against it.

Human growth

Humans start growing at fertilisation. The **gestation period** is the time of growth between fertilisation and birth.

The gestation period is different for other mammals. Usually, the larger the animal, the longer the gestation period.

During gestation parts of the body grow at different rates. The next diagram shows the relative growth of body parts of a human.

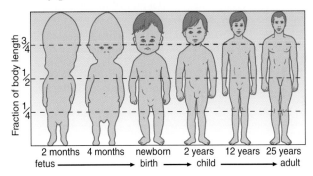

The graphs show data on weight and head size in babies. The data can provide doctors with early warnings of growth problems.

If a baby's measurements fall inside the normal range then there is no cause for concern.

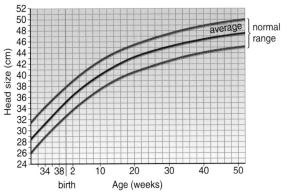

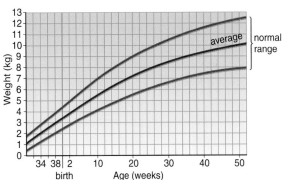

1 Why are stem cells easier to find in an embryo than an adult?

2 Explain how the process of meiosis is different to mitosis.

3 Describe how plant and animal growth are different.

4 Look at the graphs of weight and head size on page 9.

   (a) What is the normal weight range for a 30-week-old baby?
   (b) A 20-week-old baby has a head measurement of 48 cm. What does this mean?

5 Look at the diagram of body proportions on page 9. What proportion of the body is the head:

   (a) at two months old   (b) at two years old?

B3f Controlling plant growth & B3g New genes for old

After revising these items you should:

- be able to explain how plant growth and responses are controlled by growth regulators (hormones) and can be controlled by humans, and explain mutations, selective breeding and arguments for and against genetic engineering.

Plant hormones

Plants show growth responses to light and gravity.

Response	Result
positive	plant grows **towards** an environmental stimulus
negative	plant grows **away** from an environmental stimulus

Part of plant	Response to light	Response to gravity
shoot	positively phototropic	negatively geotropic
root	negatively phototropic	positively geotropic

The main hormone plants produce is **auxin**. Plants respond to hormones produced as a result of environmental stimuli – these growth responses are called tropisms.

The diagram shows how auxin affects growth.

Auxin made in the tip of the shoot diffuses away from the tip. It causes the cells to grow more and become elongated.

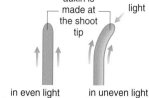

auxin is made at the shoot tip — light

in even light the auxin passes down the shoot and causes even growth

in uneven light the auxin causes more growth on the shaded side of the shoot

- In even light, auxin causes even growth so the shoot grows straight upwards.

- In uneven light, auxin accumulates on the shaded side of the shoot. Cells on this side grow more than cells on the light side so the shoot curves towards the light.

Horticulturalists use **plant hormones** to improve their crops. Scientists have produced artificial hormones which mimic the real ones.

The commercial uses of hormones include:

- **selective weedkillers** to kill only the unwanted plants
- **rooting powders** to encourage root growth in cuttings
- fruit ripening so that fruit can be picked unripe and ripened during transportation
- control of **dormancy** so that plants can be produced on demand.

How science works

There is greater demand for flowers at special times of the year, e.g. Mother's Day. Scientists have used developments in plant hormone knowledge to achieve flowering whenever they want.

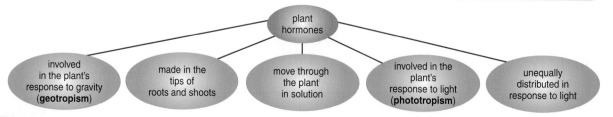

plant hormones

involved in the plant's response to gravity (**geotropism**)

made in the tips of roots and shoots

move through the plant in solution

involved in the plant's response to light (**phototropism**)

unequally distributed in response to light

Mutation

Mutations are changes to genes. They can be beneficial but most are harmful. A mutation changes the DNA base sequence in the gene. This changes or prevents the production of the protein the gene normally codes for.

The causes of mutations include:

- radiation
- chemicals

or they may occur spontaneously.

Normally mutations occur at a very slow rate.

Humans cannot change the genes of organisms by causing mutations – the results would be random. Instead we have been genetically modifying organisms:

- by selective breeding over thousands of years, and
- more recently, using genetic engineering.

Selective breeding

We can use **selective breeding** to choose favourable characteristics in a plant or animal.

The process involves these stages:

1 Select the desired characteristic, e.g. horses that run fast, sheep with more wool.

2 Choose a male and a female with the desired characteristic and breed them together. (If they come from different species we call this **cross-breeding**.)

3 Choose two of the offspring with the desired characteristic and breed them together.

4 Repeat the process for many generations until the animal with the desired characteristic is produced.

Selective breeding over many generations can create problems:

- A reduction in the gene pool and less variation.
- Repeated **inbreeding** can lead to an accumulation of harmful recessive characteristics.

Genetic engineering

Scientists can transfer genes from one living organism to another to give the recipient organism new characteristics. This is called **genetic engineering** (or genetic modification).

The following table shows the principles of genetic engineering, with an example.

Principle	Example – insulin production
select characteristic	identify the insulin gene
isolate gene	isolate the gene from a human chromosome
insert gene	insert human insulin gene into a bacterium
replicate	the bacterium replicates and makes more bacteria containing the insulin gene
	the bacteria produce human insulin

The diagram shows these principles.

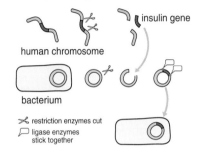

Another example of genetic engineering is taking genes from carrots that control beta-carotene production and putting them into rice. Humans eat rice and can convert the beta-carotene in the rice into Vitamin A.

This means that people in those parts of the world where the diet is lacking in Vitamin A, can now get the vitamin from their diet.

Benefits and risks of genetic engineering

There are both advantages and risks to moving genes between organisms. For example it allows us to produce organisms with new features that are useful to humans. But an inserted gene could have unexpected harmful effects.

Benefits:	Risks:
• We can produce organisms with desired characteristics quickly.	• Inserted genes may have harmful effects on the organism.
• We can modify plants to be resistant to disease, frost damage or to be **pesticide** resistant.	• Genes may be harmful to the environment if they escape.
• We can produce chemicals needed by humans (e.g. insulin) without the need to kill animals.	• Potential side effects of genetically modified food on human health.

Test yourself

1   Why is it important that a shoot is positively phototropic?

2   These diagrams show six shoots in different conditions.

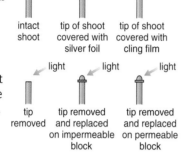

For each diagram draw what the shoot would look like after two days. Explain each answer.

3   Production of human insulin and beta-carotene are applications of genetic engineering. Give another example.

4   Gordon cuts the tip off a shoot, places the tip on an agar block and leaves it for two days. He then throws away the tip and places the agar block on the stump of the original shoot. Describe and explain what he will observe.

B3h More of the same

After revising this item you should:

● be able to explain how to create genetically identical copies of complex animals by cloning, understand the advantages and disadvantages of using cloned plants and explain tissue culture as a means of cloning plants.

Cloning animals

A **clone** is a genetically identical copy of an organism.

Identical twins are naturally occurring clones. So are organisms produced by asexual reproduction.

One way humans can clone animals is by using embryo transplants. This has been done in cows. The process copies what happens when identical twins are produced.

The offspring will be identical to each other but not to either of the parents. This is because the original fertilised egg came from sexual reproduction, so there is a mixture of genes from both parents.

The diagram below shows the steps involved in cloning cows.

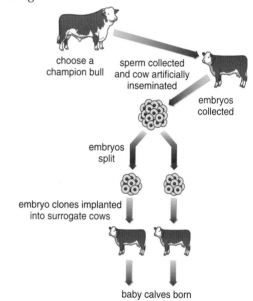

choose a champion bull / sperm collected and cow artificially inseminated / embryos collected / embryos split / embryo clones implanted into surrogate cows / baby calves born

The first mammal to be cloned from an adult mammal was Dolly the sheep in 1996. The diagram below shows the method used to clone Dolly.

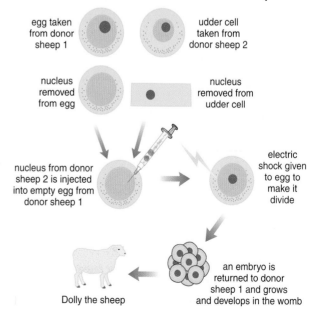

egg taken from donor sheep 1 / udder cell taken from donor sheep 2 / nucleus removed from egg / nucleus removed from udder cell / nucleus from donor sheep 2 is injected into empty egg from donor sheep 1 / electric shock given to egg to make it divide / an embryo is returned to donor sheep 1 and grows and develops in the womb / Dolly the sheep

How science works

Scientists can clone animals that have had a human gene inserted by genetic engineering. For example they could be cloned to produce a human protein such as insulin. They could also be used as a supply of organs for human transplants.

What are the implications of using cloned animals to supply replacement organs for humans?

The following table shows some of the issues involved in animal cloning.

Benefits:	Risks:
• Stem cells could be used for treating illness. • Animals could be used as a supply of organs for transplant.	• If all the animals are identical they could all be killed by one pathogenic organism. • Animal diseases could spread to humans. • The practice could lead to human cloning.

The possibility of cloning humans raises ethical dilemmas:

- It would involve killing human embryos, which some people believe is unacceptable.
- Would the cloned child, with the same genes as someone else, be a true individual?

Cloning plants

Plant cloning has been happening for thousands of years.

- Some plants make clones of themselves by asexual reproduction, e.g. the spider plant.
- Gardeners take cuttings of plants to produce new ones.

A more modern method of cloning uses **tissue culture**:

1 Select a plant for a specific characteristic.
2 Cut the plant into many small pieces.
3 Grow pieces on suitable growth medium, containing correct nutrients.
4 Use sterile conditions to avoid infection (**aseptic technique**).
5 Pieces grow into new plants that are genetically identical to the original one.

The following table shows the advantages and disadvantages of producing cloned plants commercially.

Advantages	Disadvantages
you know what you are going to get because all the plants will be genetically identical to each other and to the parent	the population of plants will be genetically very similar – there will be little variety
you can mass produce plants that do not flower very often or are difficult to grow from seeds	because the plants are very similar, a disease or change in the environment could wipe out all of them

Plant cloning is easier than animal cloning because many plant cells retain the ability to differentiate (develop into different types of cells). Animal cells usually lose this ability at a very early stage.

Test yourself

1 Why might farmers want to clone animals?

2 Why is plant cloning easier than animal cloning?

3 Look at the diagram showing embryo transplants in cows (page 12).

   (a) Explain why the calves are clones of each other.

   (b) Why aren't the calves clones of either parent?

4 Many people are against animal cloning. Explain two reasons why they think it is unacceptable.

5 Look at the section on tissue culture (above).

   (a) Why are the new plants identical to the original plant?

   (b) What is in the growth medium?

   (c) Why are sterile conditions used?

B4a Who planted that there?

Leaf structure

Leaves are all different shapes, sizes and colours. However, they all:

- have the same basic structure
- carry out photosynthesis – their main job.

Although leaves have many colours they all contain the green pigment **chlorophyll**. This traps sunlight and produces food for the plant.

Leaves vary in colour because of the combination of different pigments. In autumn, chlorophyll is the first pigment to break down, which reveals the other pigments: red, orange and yellow. This is why the leaves have so many different colours during this season.

The following diagram shows the internal structure of a thin section of a leaf.

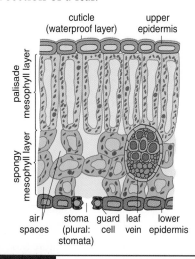

cuticle (waterproof layer)
upper epidermis
palisade mesophyll layer
spongy mesophyll layer
air spaces
stoma (plural: stomata)
guard cell
leaf vein
lower epidermis

Exam tip

You need to know the positions of the different structures shown in the diagram – you may be asked to label one like this.

There are no cells in the **cuticle**. It is a layer of wax which helps to prevent water loss.

Under the cuticle are different layers of cells. Every cell in these layers has the same features as a typical plant cell. Some cells have chloroplasts which contain chlorophyll to trap sunlight energy.

Leaves and photosynthesis

The raw materials for photosynthesis are:

- carbon dioxide – from the air
- water – from the soil.

Photosynthesis produces a sugar called glucose. This is:

- used for respiration
- converted into other substances for storage or use in the cell.

Photosynthesis also produces oxygen, which is released to the air or used in respiration.

Exam tip

You need to know:

- *the equations for photosynthesis*
- *where the raw materials come from*
- *what the waste products can be used for. Remember, the word and symbol equations are:*

$$\text{carbon dioxide} + \text{water} \longrightarrow \text{glucose} + \text{oxygen}$$
$$6CO_2 + 6H_2O \longrightarrow C_6H_{12}O_6 + 6O_2$$

Leaves are adapted in many ways for photosynthesis. The table shows this.

Feature	Adaptation
broad	gives large surface area to absorb sunlight
thin	provides short distance for gases to diffuse
chloroplasts	they contain chlorophyll to trap sunlight
veins	help to support the leaf and transport substances around it
stomata	allow gases to diffuse in and out through the **lower epidermis**

Efficient photosynthesis

The leaf is also adapted at the cellular level to improve the efficiency of photosynthesis.

Structure	Adaptation
transparent **upper epidermis** (no chloroplasts)	allows light to pass straight through to the **palisade mesophyll** layer below
palisade mesophyll is near the top	contains the most chloroplasts to trap light energy and photosynthesise
air spaces in the **spongy mesophyll**	allows diffusion of gases between the stomata and the photosynthesising cells in the mesophyll layers
very large internal surface area to volume ratio	gives more surface area for absorption of carbon dioxide from air spaces
guard cells	control the opening and closing of stomata for the entry and release of gases

How science works

Some organisms can produce food without photosynthesising – they use hydrogen sulphide instead of water. Scientists are hoping to use them to produce food in the future.

Test yourself

1 How do the products of photosynthesis get to the rest of the plant?

2 In what parts of the leaf does diffusion take place?

3 Look at the diagram of the internal structure of a leaf (page 14).
   (a) Why are there no chloroplasts in the upper epidermis?
   (b) Where does most photosynthesis take place? Give a reason for your answer.
   (c) Which layer allows the gases to circulate? Give a reason for your answer.

4 Explain why trees with needles are not as efficient at photosynthesis as those with broad leaves.

B4b Water, water everywhere

After revising this item you should:

● be able to explain osmosis, understand the role of water movement and transpiration in plants and explain how a plant attempts to reduce water loss.

Osmosis

Osmosis is a special type of diffusion.

Osmosis is:

• the net movement of water molecules (water molecules move in both directions but more move in one direction than the other)

• from an area of high water concentration (dilute solution)

• to an area of low water concentration (concentrated solution)

• across a **partially permeable** membrane

• due to the random movement of particles.

A high concentration of water is usually referred to as a high water potential.

A partially permeable membrane is one that allows certain substances (small water molecules) to pass across it, but not others (large molecules).

The following diagram shows the molecular movement in osmosis.

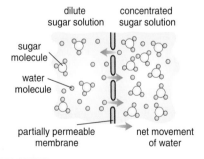

Exam tip

Make sure you understand that dilute solutions contain high water concentrations and vice versa. Think about adding water to concentrated squash to dilute it.

Predicting osmosis

You can predict which way water molecules will move if you know the concentrations of the solutions on either side of a partially permeable membrane.

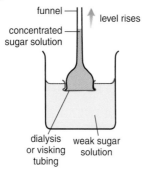

The following diagram shows two sugar solutions separated by dialysis tubing. As the solution in the beaker contains more water, the water will leave the beaker and pass into the funnel.

Water is important to plants because it helps to support them.

- The contents of the turgid cells push against the inelastic cell walls.
- This turgor pressure helps to support the cell.
- When there is little or no turgor pressure, the plant **wilts**.

When plants cells are full of water, the cells are **turgid**. When the plant wilts and the cells are short of water they are **flaccid**.

If a plant loses too much water, the cell membrane may pull away from the cell wall. We call this **plasmolysis**. A plasmolysed cell cannot return to being turgid and usually dies.

Water movement and transpiration

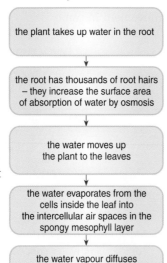

The diagram opposite shows the stages in water movement through a plant.

Transpiration is the loss of water vapour from a leaf. Leaves have to open their stomata to allow gases in and out for efficient photosynthesis. Water diffuses out as well.

The rate of transpiration changes when environmental conditions change.

Transpiration provides plants with water for:

- cooling (as evaporation needs heat energy which comes from the leaf)
- photosynthesis (water is a raw material)
- support (turgor pressure)
- movement of **minerals** (dissolved in the water).

Plants and their leaves function well when they are turgid, so they try not to lose excessive water. The leaf structure helps with this. It has:

- a waxy cuticle
- few stomata on the upper surface (where evaporation is greatest)
- control over the opening of the stomata.

Stomata

The stomata have two guard cells on either side. These can change their shape and open or close the pore (stoma) between them.

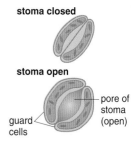

They work like this:

- When there is a lot of light, and plenty of water, the guard cells take in water and become turgid. The inner walls of the guard cells bend and the stoma opens.
- In low light, or with water in short supply, the opposite happens and the stoma closes.

Plants that live in the desert have very few stomata on both leaf surfaces, to minimise water loss in the dry desert conditions. The size of the stomata is usually small when compared to plants that live where water is readily available.

How science works

Plant scientists investigate the number of stomata on different leaves and on the different surfaces of leaves. They collect and analyse the data to provide evidence for models and theories to explain why there are different numbers of stomata on different leaves.

This leads them to understand why plants grow in different places. Those with fewer stomata are found in drier places because they do not lose as much water through their stomata.

Animal cells and water

Animal cells also take in water by osmosis.

- If they take in too much water the cell membrane bursts, as they lack the inelastic cell wall to resist the pressure. This is called **lysis**.
- If they lose too much water, they shrivel up. This is **crenation**.

Test yourself

1 Explain how osmosis is different to diffusion.

2 Why do cooks put cleaned vegetables in water during preparation?

3 A plant wilts after it is dug up and replanted. Which structures must have been removed?

4 Ben weighs three identical pieces of celery and places them into three different solutions. After four hours he takes them out, blots them dry and weighs them again. Ben finds that one is heavier, one is lighter and one remains the same mass.

    (a) Name the process that had taken place.
    (b) Explain why the pieces of celery have different masses.

5 Where in a potato is the partially permeable membrane that water passes through during osmosis?

B4c Transport in plants & B4d Plants need minerals too

After revising these items you should:

- be able to explain the structure and arrangement of xylem and phloem, explain how different factors change the rate of transpiration, understand what plants need minerals for and explain what happens if they are short of these minerals.

How are materials transported?

The plant has two transport systems:

- The **xylem**.
- The **phloem**.

The following diagram shows how the xylem and the phloem are arranged in a leaf, stem and root.

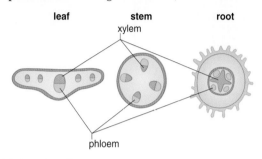

Exam tip

In the stem and root, xylem is always in the middle.

Water always moves up the xylem. Dissolved sugars can move up or down the phloem. The movement of sugars in the phloem is called **translocation**.

Xylem vessels and phloem tubes run continuously throughout the leaves, stems and roots of a plant. In the stem they are gathered together into clusters called **vascular bundles**.

What is transported?

Plants transport many different materials up and down their stems and roots. The table shows some of these and their movements.

What is transported	What is it transported in	Where is it picked up	Where is it going
water	xylem vessels	roots (from the soil)	shoots and leaves
minerals	xylem vessels	roots (dissolved in water from the soil)	shoots and leaves
sugar	phloem tubes	leaves or storage areas	growing and storage tissues

These tissues are specially designed to carry out their functions:

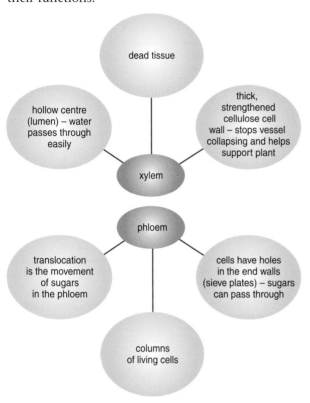

Transpiration rate increases with:	Why it increases?
increased light intensity	there is more photosynthesis so the stomata are open for gas exchange and water diffuses out
increased temperature	molecules have more kinetic energy so evaporate faster
increase in air movement	if it is windy water vapour gets blown away so the concentration gradient is maintained and more vapour diffuses out
decrease in humidity (linked to increased air movement)	the concentration gradient allows more vapour to diffuse out

Exam tip

*Remember that transpiration is the evaporation of **water vapour** from the surfaces of the cells and its diffusion down a water potential gradient from a high water potential (usually inside the leaf) to a low water potential (usually outside the leaf).*

How science works

Growing food for humans to eat is now a big business which requires carefully controlled conditions. These are often provided in glasshouses which use technology to monitor and control environmental conditions such as temperature, carbon dioxide and water levels.

Transpiration rate

During transpiration, water evaporates into the air spaces in the leaf and diffuses out through the stomata. Transpiration creates a suction force that helps to pull more water up through the xylem vessels from the roots.

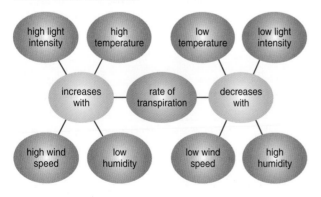

Minerals: what's needed?

Humans need minerals in their diet in order to grow properly. Plants do as well.

Humans get their minerals from their food. Plants get their minerals from the soil, dissolved in the water that enters the roots.

Plants photosynthesise to make sugars as their food. They need minerals to turn these sugars into proteins and DNA.

The following table shows some different minerals and how plants use them.

Element required	Main source	Used by plants to produce:
magnesium	magnesium compounds	chlorophyll for photosynthesis
nitrogen	nitrates	amino acids for making proteins which are needed for cell growth
phosphorus	phosphates	DNA and cell membranes to make new cells for respiration and growth
potassium	potassium compounds	compounds needed to help enzymes in photosynthesis and respiration

Deficiency diseases

Mineral **deficiencies** lead to poor plant growth. The next table shows the effect of mineral deficiencies on growth.

Mineral	Effect of deficiency on growth
magnesium	yellow leaves
nitrate	poor growth and yellow leaves
phosphate	poor root growth and discoloured leaves
potassium	poor flower and fruit growth and discoloured leaves

We can set up experiments to show that mineral deficiency leads to poor growth. The apparatus is shown in the following diagram.

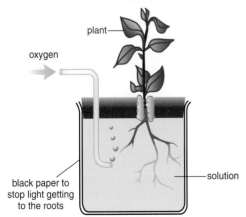

plant

oxygen

solution

black paper to stop light getting to the roots

Several beakers of solution are used:
- One has all minerals the plant needs.
- Each of the others is deficient in one mineral.

Minerals are usually present in the soil in low concentrations. Their concentrations are higher in the roots than in the soil – so they cannot diffuse into the root hairs.

The plants must move these minerals against their concentration gradient instead, using **active transport**. This requires energy, which comes from respiration, so roots need lots of oxygen to respire.

Test yourself

1 How can you show that water is transported up the stem of a plant?

2 This diagram shows a potometer. It is a device for measuring the uptake of water by a leafy shoot.

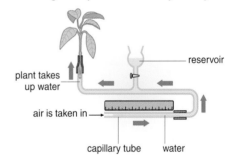

reservoir

plant takes up water

air is taken in

capillary tube   water

(a) After 20 minutes the water has moved along the capillary tube. Which way will it move? Explain your answer.
(b) The water moves 30 mm in 20 minutes. Calculate the speed of movement in millimetres per minute.
(c) If the apparatus was placed in windy conditions, would the water move faster or slower? Explain your answer.

3 What quantitative method would you use to show that water is lost from a plant, using the following apparatus: potted plant, digital scales, polythene?

4 How do some plants get help from other plants in obtaining their minerals?

5 Why do plants need to use energy to take up minerals from the soil?

B4e Energy flow

After revising this item you should:

● be able to explain pyramids of numbers and biomass, how the efficiency of energy transfer between organisms shapes them, and how we can transfer the energy in biomass.

Pyramids

All living organisms need energy. Ultimately this energy comes from the Sun.

This energy:

● is absorbed by plants and enters food chains
● flows through food webs and whole ecosystems
● is harnessed by humans, e.g. for agriculture.

The following diagram shows a simple food chain.

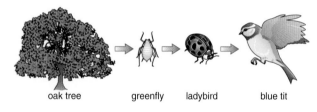

| oak tree | greenfly | ladybird | blue tit |

The producer is the first organism in every food chain. All the other organisms in the chain are consumers.

The food chain shows which organisms consume which other organisms, but it does not give us any information on how many organisms there are at each stage.

Instead we can draw a **pyramid of numbers**.

1 Count the number of organisms at each stage (**trophic level**) of the food chain.

2 Draw a box to scale to represent these numbers.

The pyramid of numbers does not take into account the size of each organism. For this we need to construct a **pyramid of biomass**. This shows the mass of living material at each stage of the food chain or food web.

The next diagram shows two pyramids.

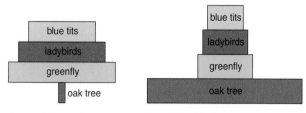

Pyramid of numbers.   *Pyramid of biomass.*

In the pyramid of numbers the oak tree is shown as a small box as it is only one tree. In the pyramid of biomass the oak tree is shown as a large box because it has a large mass of living material.

Energy in food chains

Energy from the Sun flows through food chains by:

● photosynthesis   ● feeding

Photosynthesis produces glucose. When consumers eat plants the energy locked up in the glucose passes to the animal. The energy passes from consumer to consumer as each organism feeds.

Some of the energy is transferred to less useful forms of energy at each trophic level. This leaves the food chain by:

● heat from respiration
● **egestion** (waste material from a cell or organism).

The following diagram shows how energy moves through a food chain.

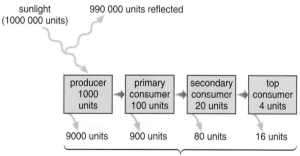

Look back at the pyramid of biomass at the top of the page. The efficiency of energy transfer explains its shape. The more energy is lost at any trophic level, the less energy there is to be passed to the next stage.

This loss of energy also explains why food chains rarely contain more than five or six organisms. There is not enough energy left at the end to support more levels.

Energy from biomass

Humans can harness and use the energy in plant **biomass** (the mass of living material) in different ways.

Here are some ways of transferring energy from biomass:

- burn wood from fast growing trees
- ferment biomass using yeast to produce alcohol
- ferment biomass using bacteria to produce biogas.

There are several reasons for developing these **biofuels**:

- Renewable – they do not run out.
- Reduce air pollution by carbon dioxide.
- Provide energy self-reliance to countries that do not have fossil fuel reserves.

Humans can choose to use biomass in many ways. They can:

- use it as fuel • eat it • feed it to animals
- grow it (seeds) to make more plants.

B4f Farming

Intensive farming

Many farmers try to produce as much food as possible from the amount of land, plants and animals available. They use **intensive farming** methods to achieve this.

Intensive farming methods of food production improve the efficiency of energy transfer. They do this by reducing the energy transferred (or lost):

- to pests • to competing plants.

Intensive farming also reduces energy lost as heat as animals are kept in pens indoors. Our use of these methods can raise ethical dilemmas. They may be efficient and produce more food – but they also can lead to environmental problems.

For example, pesticides:

- can harm useful organisms, like plant-pollinating insects
- can enter the food chain – sometimes the pesticides do not break down and as they accumulate (build up) in animals higher up the food chain, they may kill them.

The next diagram shows how this happens.

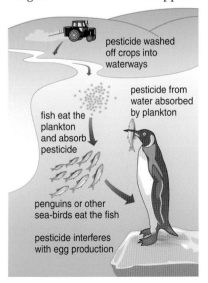

pesticide washed off crops into waterways

pesticide from water absorbed by plankton

fish eat the plankton and absorb pesticide

penguins or other sea-birds eat the fish

pesticide interferes with egg production

Soil-free farming

Plants are usually grown in soil, but not always. Growing plants without soil is becoming increasingly popular. The technique is known as **hydroponics**.

Crops are sometimes grown in artificial soil or in water. This is particularly useful for growing tomatoes in glasshouses or where the soil is very poor. The next table shows some of the advantages and disadvantages of hydroponics.

Advantages	Disadvantages
better control of mineral levels	lack of support for the plant
better control of disease	need to add fertilisers

Organic farming

Organic farming has become more widespread recently (although intensive farming techniques are still far more common). Organic farming is where no artificial fertilisers, pesticides or herbicides are added to the soil.

The table shows the function of each of these chemicals.

Chemical	Function
fertiliser	adds minerals to help plant growth
pesticides (including insecticides and fungicides)	kill pests: • insecticides kill insects • fungicides kill fungi
herbicides	kill plants (weeds)

Many different techniques are used in organic farming:

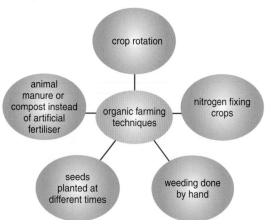

Organic farming has many benefits but it also has some disadvantages.

Advantages	Disadvantages
no artificial chemicals which can harm the environment	labour intensive – crops weeded by hand
possible health benefits of organic food to humans	organic food costs more in the shops
allows varied seed planting times and crop rotation to avoid diseases	

Biological control

Pesticides kill pests. Organic farming uses natural methods to control pests instead of artificial pesticides. Natural methods are those that use living organisms to control the pests. The organism is usually a predator that eats the pest.

The table shows some advantages and disadvantages of **biological control**.

Advantages	Disadvantages
the control organism only kills the pest	sometimes the control organism can become a pest itself
no artificial pesticides are needed	if the pest is wiped out, other organisms higher in the food chain may die through lack of food

We need to be careful when using biological control techniques. Removing a pest from a food chain or food web can cause problems for other organisms because their food source is removed.

Test yourself

1 Explain why battery farming of chickens is an example of intensive farming. How does battery farming reduce energy lost by the chickens?

2 How does crop rotation help organic farming?

3 Give an example of biological control.

4 Use this table to answer the questions.

Organism	What they eat	Molecules of insecticide in their body
aphid	plant sap containing ten molecules of insecticide	10
ladybird	100 aphids	
thrush	1000 ladybirds	
sparrowhawk	2000 thrushes	

    (a)   Calculate how much insecticide each organism contains and fill in the table.

    (b)   How much more insecticide is in the sparrowhawk's body compared with the aphid?

    (c)   Why does the insecticide harm the thrush but not the aphid?

B4g Decay & B4h Recycling

After revising these items you should:

- understand what decay is, what causes it and what affects its rate, explain how food is preserved, understand the carbon and nitrogen cycles and explain how bacteria contribute to the recycling of nitrogen.

Causes of decay

All organisms are made of organic material and when organisms die this breaks down. This is the process of **decay**.

If decay did not happen then all the dead organisms would remain. Decay releases the nutrients from their bodies and these can be recycled.

The following table shows how different conditions affect the rate of decay.

temperature	warmer conditions allow more decay because they favour the growth and reproduction of microorganisms that cause decay
amount of oxygen	microorganisms need oxygen to respire aerobically so the rate of decay is greater when oxygen is plentiful
amount of water	microorganisms need water to dissolve substances and to respire – if the conditions are too dry, there will be no decay

The ideal conditions for decay are the presence of warmth, oxygen and water. Without these, decay slows down.

Decomposers and detritivores

Two main groups of organisms bring about decay.

decomposers (e.g. bacteria and fungi)	• these organisms are **saprophytes** • they release enzymes onto the dead organisms then absorb the partially digested material • this is **saprophytic** feeding
detritivores (e.g. earthworms, maggots and woodlice)	• these organisms help the decomposers • they feed on the dead and decaying material (**detritus**) and break it down into smaller pieces with a larger surface area for decomposers to work on

Every autumn the leaves fall from the trees. Why have they disappeared by the following spring?

1 Detrivores eat the leaves and earthworms pull them into the soil. This starts the breakdown process.

2 Decomposers in the soil continue the breakdown.

3 Chemicals in the leaves are released into the soil and taken up by roots to be reused by plants the following year.

In some conditions, e.g. waterlogged soils with no oxygen, decay is restricted so the nutrients are not available to the plant roots.

Food preservation

All organic material decays but sometimes we want to delay this process. For example, fruit needs to be kept fresh and free from decay.

To prevent or reduce the rate of decay, various methods of **food preservation** can be used. The following table shows some preservation methods and how they prevent decay.

Preservation method	How decay is prevented
canning	the high temperature kills the microorganisms water and oxygen cannot get into the can after it is sealed
cooling	the low temperature slows down the growth and respiration of microorganisms
drying	microorganisms cannot respire or reproduce
freezing	microorganisms cannot respire or reproduce because their chemical reactions are slowed down
adding salt or sugar	the sugar or salt draws water out of the microorganisms
adding vinegar	the vinegar is too acidic for the microorganisms preventing their enzymes from working

How science works

Food preservation means that we can now transport food over large distances without it going off. For instance, fresh fruit and vegetables can be flown in from countries in Africa.

Some people are concerned about 'food miles' – how far the food has been transported to reach us – because this releases carbon dioxide which contributes to global warming.

But growing fruit and vegetables to export is an important source of income to poor people in developing countries, so making an ethical choice when buying food can be difficult.

Recycling

Recycling is nothing new. Bacteria and fungi have been recycling nutrients for millions of years. They decompose dead animals and plants, releasing the nutrients so that they are available for living plants and animals to take in.

If this did not take place living organisms would not have a supply of carbon and nitrogen. These two elements are the most commonly recycled and you need to know about the carbon and nitrogen cycles.

The carbon cycle

Carbon is the basic element that makes up the molecules that build organisms. It is found in carbohydrates, proteins and fats.

The main source of carbon is from the carbon dioxide in the air.

- This is incorporated into living organisms when plants photosynthesis.
- Carbon is trapped in carbon compounds, which are passed along food chains and food webs.
- Carbon returns to the air as carbon dioxide when animals and plants respire.
- Soil bacteria and fungi (decomposers) release carbon dioxide into the air during aerobic respiration.

The carbon cycle is shown in the next diagram.

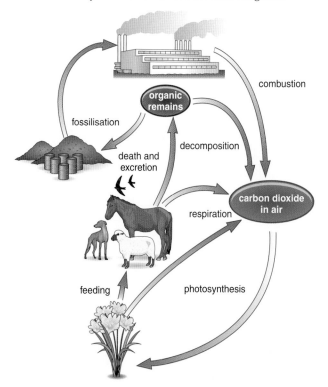

Another part of the carbon cycle is the making and burning of fossil fuels. Some organisms may not decay and become fossils instead. They are compressed underground and turn into fuels. Burning releases the carbon trapped in these fuels.

Carbon is also recycled in the sea:

1 Marine organisms make shells out of **carbonates**. Carbonates contain carbon.

2 The organisms die and their shells fall to the sea bed.

3 These are compressed and turn into limestone.

4 The limestone gets worn away by weathering or by volcanic activity.

5 Carbon dioxide is released into the air and joins the cycle again.

The nitrogen cycle

The air is made of 78 per cent nitrogen but it is too unreactive to be used by animals or plants.

Instead, plants take in nitrates from the soil to make protein for growth. These nitrogen compounds are passed along food chains and webs as organisms feed.

When animals and plants die, the compounds are broken down by decomposers back into nitrates and returned to the soil.

This is the nitrogen cycle.

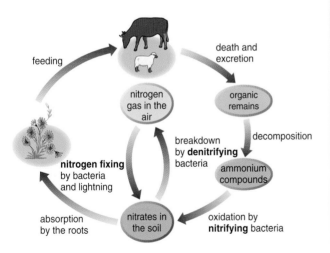

At each stage of the cycle specialised bacteria are responsible for the conversion of one nitrogen compound into another.

Type of bacteria	What they do
decomposing (live in the soil)	convert proteins from dead organisms and **urea** (waste material) into ammonia
nitrifying	convert this ammonia into nitrates
denitrifying	change nitrates back into nitrogen gas
nitrogen-fixing (live in the soil or in the root nodules of leguminous plants, e.g. clover)	remove nitrogen gas from the air (lightning also does this)

Test yourself

1 Fish can be preserved by freezing, drying and canning.

   (a) What do these methods have in common?
   (b) How are the three methods different?

2 A warden on a nature reserve notices that the egg shells of some birds are damaged by pesticides. But the reserve where the birds live is not polluted with pesticides. Explain why the birds' eggs are affected.

3 How do leguminous plants help to recycle nitrogen?

4 Making compost is encouraged by local councils. Waste material such as vegetable peelings, leaves and grass are ideal for the compost heap.

   (a) What living organisms need to be in the compost heap for decay to occur?
   (b) Sometimes water is added to compost. Explain why.
   (c) Why do gardeners usually turn their compost heaps?

5 Explain why respiration and photosynthesis are important in the carbon cycle.

C3a What are atoms like?

After revising this item you should:

- be able to describe what is inside an atom, the connection between electronic structure and the Periodic Table and the structure of isotopes.

Atomic structure

An **atom** is made up from:

- **electrons** – arranged around the nucleus in a number of electron shells which are further and further out from the nucleus
- **protons** and **neutrons** – in the nucleus in the centre of the atom. The only atom that does not have any neutrons is the simplest form of hydrogen.

This diagram shows the structure of a sodium atom.

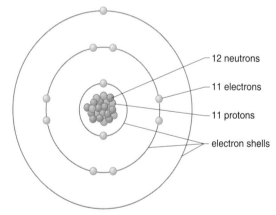

- 12 neutrons
- 11 electrons
- 11 protons
- electron shells

Inside a sodium atom.

Electrons, protons and neutrons have different properties.

Particle	Where found	Relative mass (mass compared with a proton)	Relative charge
proton	in nucleus	1	+1
neutron	in nucleus	1	0
electron	outside nucleus	0.0005	−1

The atom is neutral because the number of protons (positive charges) equals the number of electrons (negative charges).

How science works

In 1807, John Dalton stated that atoms were like hard balls that could not be broken down. In 1897, Joseph Thompson found electrons inside the atom.

How do these two ideas conflict with each other?

Atomic number and mass number

The **atomic number** is the number of protons in an atom. The **mass number** is the total number of protons plus neutrons in an atom.

The shorthand way of writing an atom to show the number of nuclear particles is to put the mass number at the top left and the atomic number at the bottom left of the symbol. So $^{27}_{13}$Al shows that an atom of aluminium has 13 protons and 27 − 13 = 14 neutrons.

Isotopes

Each atom of the same element has the same number of protons. But in many elements some of the atoms have different numbers of neutrons.

Atoms of the same element with different mass numbers are called **isotopes**.

Because mass number is number of protons + neutrons, isotopes are also atoms of the same element that have different numbers of neutrons. The table shows the number of protons and neutrons in two isotopes of chlorine.

Isotope	Chlorine-35	Chlorine-37
number of protons	17	17
number of neutrons	18	20
mass number	35	37

Exam tip

You can find the number of neutrons by subtracting the proton number from the mass number.

From this information you can work out the number of protons (and therefore electrons).

Isotopes can be written using the atomic symbols.

We can write chlorine-37 as $^{37}_{17}Cl$. The relative molecular mass of chlorine is 35.5 because natural chlorine is a mixture of 75 per cent chlorine-35 and 25 per cent chlorine-37.

Test yourself

1 An atom of phosphorus has 15 protons and 16 neutrons. What is the mass number of this phosphorus atom?

2 Work out how many protons, neutrons and electrons there are in these particles:

(a) $^{65}_{30}Zn$

(b) $^{108}_{47}Ag$

(c) $^{39}_{19}K$.

3 Two isotopes of bromine are $^{79}_{35}Br$ and $^{81}_{35}Br$. State three things that are the same in both these atoms and one thing that is different.

4 Write the symbol for the isotope of calcium which has 26 neutrons.

C3b Ionic bonding & C3c Covalent bonding and the Periodic Table

After revising these items you should:

- be able to describe how ionic and covalent compounds are formed, explain their properties and describe how the electronic structure of an atom is related to the Periodic Table.

Ionic bonding

Positive ions:

- Formed when an atom loses one or more electrons.
- E.g. sodium forms a sodium ion when a sodium atom loses one electron (e^- is the symbol for an electron).

$$Na - e^- \rightarrow Na^+$$

- E.g. magnesium forms a magnesium ion when a magnesium atom loses two electrons.

$$Mg - 2e^- \rightarrow Mg^{2+}$$

Negative ions:

- Formed when an atom gains one or more electrons.
- E.g. chlorine forms a chloride ion when a chlorine atom gains one electron.

$$Cl + e^- \rightarrow Cl^-$$

- E.g. oxygen forms an oxide ion when an oxygen atom gains two electrons.

$$O + 2e^- \rightarrow O^{2-}$$

When a metal combines with a non-metal, one or more electrons move from the metal atom to the non-metal atom. The positive and negative ions formed then attract each other. This attraction between positive and negative charges forms the **ionic bond**.

Exam tip

Remember that a covalent compound is formed between non-metals only. An ionic compound is formed between a metal and a non-metal.

Dot and cross diagrams for ionic bonding

The transfer of electrons from the metal atom to the non-metal atom always results in both ions having a complete outer shell. This is called a **stable octet**.

Each ion formed has the same electron arrangement as a noble gas:

- Neon arrangement for the sodium ion.
- Argon arrangement for the chloride ion.

We can use dots and crosses to represent electrons and show how the ions are formed.

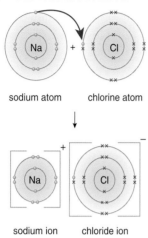

Dot and cross diagram for sodium chloride.

You need to work out the following dot and cross diagrams.

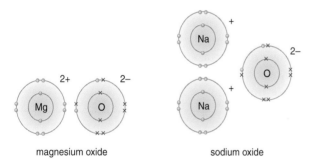

magnesium oxide   sodium oxide

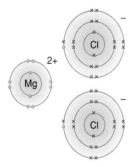

magnesium chloride

From ions to formulae

You can use the charges on the ions to work out the formulae of **ionic compounds**. The total positive charge must equal the total negative charge so that there is no overall charge on the compound. For example:

- Magnesium chloride – the ions are Mg^{2+} and Cl^-. To make the charges equal you need two Cl^- ions. So the formula is $MgCl_2$.
- Sodium oxide – the ions are Na^+ and O^{2-}. You need two sodium ions for every oxide so the formula is Na_2O.

Properties of ionic compounds

The following table summarises the properties of ionic compounds, e.g. sodium chloride and magnesium oxide.

electricity conduction	do not conduct when solid – the ions cannot move
	do conduct when molten – the ions are free to move
structure	the ions are arranged regularly in a giant **ionic lattice**
	the positive and negative ions are held together by a strong **electrostatic attraction**
	The arrangement of ions in a sodium chloride lattice.
melting point	very high – a lot of energy is needed to overcome the strong electrostatic attraction between ions
	magnesium oxide has a higher melting point than sodium chloride – magnesium oxide has doubly charged ions so has stronger attraction between ions

Exam tip

Remember that conduction in ionic compounds is due to movement of ions not electrons. The electrons in the ions are firmly held in position.

How science works

Ionic nitrates (e.g. sodium nitrate) are mined by large multinational companies, often in poor countries. What financial, social and political problems have to be taken into account when considering expanding these mines?

Covalent bonding

Features of **covalent bonding** are shown in the diagram.

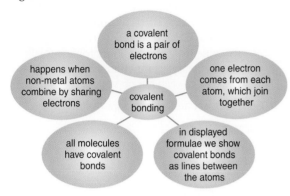

The diagram shows how covalent bond formation is represented.

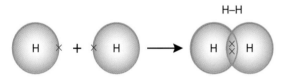

Dot and cross diagrams for covalent bonding

The diagrams below show how the pairs of electrons are shared between each atom. Each atom combines so that it has a full outer shell of eight electrons (a stable octet). The exception is hydrogen which has a full outer shell with two electrons.

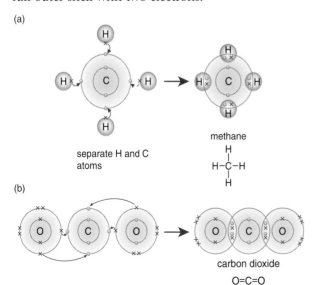

Dot and cross diagrams for covalent bonding in (a) methane and (b) carbon dioxide.

In order to get eight electrons around each atom, you sometimes have to pair up two sets of electrons to form a double bond.

Properties of molecular structures

The following table summarises the properties of simple covalent molecules, e.g. carbon dioxide and water.

electricity conduction	do not conduct – have no ions and so their electrons cannot move outside their molecules
melting point and boiling point	low – due to weak **intermolecular forces** between the **molecules** (most small molecules are gases or liquids)

The Periodic Table

The Periodic Table shows the elements in order of increasing atomic number. It gives the mass number and atomic number of each element.

The elements in the Periodic Table are arranged in columns and rows. The columns are called **Groups**. The rows are called **Periods**. All the elements in a row are in the same Period.

The diagram shows a shortened version of the Periodic Table.

1	2	3	4	5	6	7	8
1 **H** Hydrogen 1							4 **He** Helium 2
7 **Li** Lithium 3	9 **Be** Beryllium 4	11 **B** Boron 5	12 **C** Carbon 6	14 **N** Nitrogen 7	16 **O** Oxygen 8	19 **F** Fluorine 9	20 **Ne** Neon 10
23 **Na** Sodium 11	24 **Mg** Magnesium 12	27 **Al** Aluminium 13	28 **Si** Silicon 14	31 **P** Phosphorus 15	32 **S** Sulfur 16	35.5 **Cl** Chlorine 17	40 **Ar** Argon 18
39 **K** Potassium 19	40 **Ca** Calcium 20	70 **Ga** Galium 31	73 **Ge** Germanium 32	75 **As** Arsenic 33	79 **Se** Selenium 34	80 **Br** Bromine 35	84 **Kr** Krypton 36

Electronic structure

Each electron shell can hold only a certain number of electrons:

- The shell nearest the nucleus (the first shell) can hold a maximum of two electrons.
- The second and third shells can hold a maximum of eight electrons.

The shells are filled in order starting with the lowest. The table shows you how to write electronic structures.

Element	Number of electrons	Electronic structure
hydrogen	1	1
helium	2	2
lithium	3	2.1
beryllium	4	2.2
boron	5	2.3
fluorine	9	2.7
neon	10	2.8
sodium	11	2.8.1

Exam tip

You do not have to learn the electronic structures of the first 20 elements but you must be able to work them out using a Periodic Table. Remember that the number of electrons and the number of protons are the same in the neutral atom.

Electronic structure and the Periodic Table

The electronic structure of an atom shows which Group and Period it belongs to, e.g the diagram shows sodium which is in Group 1 and Period 3.

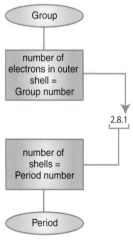

Group

number of electrons in outer shell = Group number

2.8.1

number of shells = Period number

Period

Test yourself

1 (a) Which of these substances are ionic compounds?
carbon monoxide (CO)   potassium chloride (KCl)   methane (CH_4)   magnesium chloride ($MgCl_2$)   sodium bromide (NaBr)

    (b) For each ionic compound, write down the formula of each ion present.

2 Construct dot and cross diagrams for:

    (a) water
    (b) chlorine
    (c) methane
    (d) carbon dioxide.

3 Write the formulae for:

    (a) magnesium oxide
    (b) calcium chloride
    (c) iron(III) chloride
    (d) lithium oxide.

    Use these symbols for the ions to help you:
    Mg^{2+}, Ca^{2+}, Fe^{3+}, Li^+, O^{2-}, Cl^-.

4 Molten (liquid) sodium bromide conducts electricity but water does not. Explain this difference.

5 An atom has the electronic structure 2.8.5. Which Group and Period does this atom belong to?

C3d The Group 1 elements

After revising this item you should:

- be able to explain why the Group 1 metals react in a similar way, why their reactivity increases down the Group and how to identify their ions using a flame test.

Very reactive metals

All Group 1 metals (**alkali metals**) have similar properties and react in a similar way.

As we go **down** Group 1, the metals become **more** reactive.

The difference in reactivity is best observed by comparing the reactions of small cubes of lithium, sodium and potassium with water, as shown in the diagram.

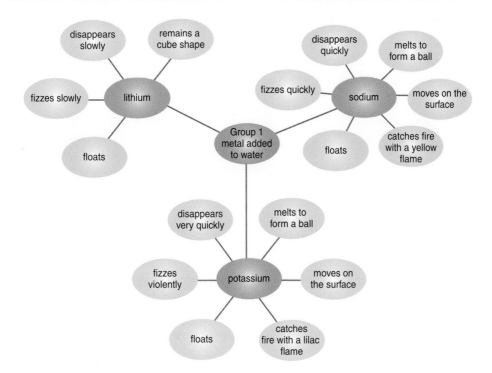

The fizzing is caused by the bubbles of hydrogen gas which are formed in this reaction. If universal indicator is added to the water, the indicator changes to purple. This shows that the reaction makes an alkali – which is why we call the Group 1 elements alkali metals.

The reason for the difference in reactivity is to do with how easy it is to lose the outer electron. The more reactive the Group 1 metal, the easier it is to lose the outer electron from an atom and form a stable ion. So the more reactive the metal, the more easily it is oxidised.

How science works

Mendeleev published his Periodic Table in 1869. Sodium and potassium were isolated in 1807 and lithium was detected in 1817.

Rubidium and caesium were not detected until 1860. Why did it take so long to detect the last two?

Predicting the properties of Group 1 metals

The properties of the Group 1 metals show trends (gradual changes) down the group. The table shows the trends in melting point, hardness and reactivity with oxygen.

You should be able to predict the properties of the other Group 1 metals from a table like this. For example, the melting point of lithium must be at least 30–40°C higher than sodium if you follow the figures.

Metal	Melting point (°C)	Hardness	Reactivity with oxygen
sodium	98	fairly soft	burns steadily when heated
potassium	64	soft	burns rapidly when heated
rubidium	39	very soft	catches fire without heating

Group 1 metals react in a similar way because:

- they all have one electron in their outer shell
- when they react, their atoms lose this electron
- an ion with a single positive charge is formed
- this ion has a stable electronic structure (full outer shell).

For sodium, the ionic equation for this 'half reaction' is written:

$$Na - e^- \rightarrow Na^+$$

We call loss of electrons **oxidation**.

You can see from the ionic equation that this is an oxidation reaction because an electron is lost.

Exam tip

Notice that the alkali metals have 'similar' chemical properties not 'the same' chemical properties. The properties change slightly as you go down the Group.

Making alkalis

The alkali formed when a Group 1 metal reacts with water is an alkali metal hydroxide, e.g. sodium hydroxide, potassium hydroxide. The alkali metal hydroxide dissolves in the water as the reaction occurs. The other product of the reaction is hydrogen.

Word equations and balanced symbol equations for the reaction of alkali metals with water follow a pattern:

$$2M + 2H_2O \rightarrow 2MOH + H_2$$
alkali metal + water → metal hydroxide + hydrogen

(where M is the alkali metal).

So the equation for the reaction between lithium and water is:

$$2Li + 2H_2O \rightarrow 2LiOH + H_2$$
lithium + water → lithium hydroxide + hydrogen

Exam tip

You only have to learn one equation for the reactions of all the alkali metals with water because they are exactly the same except for the symbol of the metal.

Flame tests

We can find out which Group 1 metal is present in an alkali metal compound by carrying out a **flame test**, as follows:

1 Moisten a flame test wire.
2 Dip the end of the wire into a sample of the solid alkali metal compound.
3 Put the sample on the wire into a blue Bunsen flame.
4 Observe the colour of the flame.

The flame test shows the alkali metal present in the alkali metal compound because each metal gives a distinctive colour.

How science works

A type of flame test can be used to identify the metal ions present in the 'black powder' in a firework.

The black powder from two fireworks was analysed. The results are shown in the table in 'parts per million' of the metal ions present.

Metal ion	Barium	Copper	Sodium
firework A	755	2050	1008
firework B	749	1870	1010

Are the fireworks the same or different? Explain why.

Test yourself

1 Look at the spider diagram showing the reaction of alkali metals with water (page 31). Describe two differences which show that potassium is more reactive that sodium.

2 Write an ionic equation to show the oxidation of potassium to potassium ions.

3 Look at the table showing the melting point, hardness and reactivity of the alkali metals (page 31). Caesium is below rubidium in Group 1. Predict caesium's melting point, hardness and reactivity with oxygen.

4 Write a word equation and a balanced symbol equation for the reaction of sodium with water.

5 State the name of the alkali formed when rubidium reacts with water.

C3e The Group 7 elements

Halogens

The elements in Group 7 of the Periodic Table are called the **halogens**. They include:

- fluorine
- chlorine
- bromine
- iodine

As you go down the Group from chlorine to iodine the halogens change in appearance. At room temperature:

- chlorine is a light green gas
- bromine is a deep orange liquid
- iodine is a grey solid.

Halogens and alkali metals

The word equations and balanced symbol equations for the reaction of halogens with alkali metals follow a pattern:

halogen + alkali metal ⟶ alkali metal **halide**

So for the reaction between potassium and chlorine:

2K	+	Cl$_2$	⟶	2KCl
potassium	+	chlorine	⟶	potassium chloride

Exam tip

Note how the name of the halogen changes in the compound. The -ine at the end of the halogen name changes to -ide when we name the compound.

For example, the element iodine is a halogen but the compound potassium iodide is an alkali metal halide.

Displacing halogens

The reactivity of the halogens decreases down the group. You can see this by looking at how halogens react with solutions of alkali metal halides. These reactions are called **displacement** reactions.

In class experiments the halogens are added as their solutions in water. The table shows the reaction between different halogens and sodium halides. The ticks show where there is a reaction.

Halogen	Halide solution		
	sodium chloride	sodium bromide	sodium iodide
chlorine	✗	✓	✓
bromine	✗	✗	✓
iodine	✗	✗	✗

You can see that the halogen reacts with the halide only when the halide is lower in the Group than the halogen.

- You can tell when there is a reaction because the colour of the solution changes.
- Alkali metal halides are colourless but the halogens are coloured.

We can write equations for these displacement reactions as follows:

Cl$_2$	+	2NaBr	⟶	Br$_2$	+	2NaCl
chlorine	+	sodium bromide	⟶	bromine	+	sodium chloride
(green)		(colourless)		(orange solution)		(colourless)

Exam tip

You only have to learn one equation for the reactions of the halogen with the halides because they follow a general pattern. Remember that the halogens are always diatomic (written with a 2 at the bottom right).

Reactivity decreases down the Group

The displacement reactions show that the halogens get less reactive as you go down the Group.

The reason for this is to do with how easy it is for a halogen atom to gain an outer electron and form a stable ion with eight outer electrons.

The more reactive the halogen, the easier it is to gain an outer electron. So the more reactive the halogen, the more easily it is reduced.

Properties of the halogens

The halogens have similar properties and react in a similar way. This is because:

- they all have seven electrons in their outer shell
- when they react, their atoms gain one electron
- an ion with a single negative charge is formed
- this ion has a stable electronic structure (full outer shell).

For chlorine, the ionic equation for this 'half reaction' is written:

$$Cl + e^- \longrightarrow Cl^-$$

Gain of electrons is called **reduction**. You can see from this ionic equation that this is a reduction reaction because an electron is gained.

Exam tip

*Use the mnemonic **OIL RIG** to remember if oxidation or reduction takes place. **O**xidation **I**s **L**oss (of electrons); **R**eduction **I**s **G**ain (of electrons).*

Predicting halogen properties

The properties of the halogens show trends (gradual changes) down the group. You should be able to predict the properties of the other halogens from a table like the following.

For example, the colour of fluorine must be lighter in colour than chlorine – it is yellow. If you follow the pattern of the figures fluorine must have a boiling point much lower than chlorine.

Halogen	Boiling point (°C)	State	Colour
chlorine	−34	gas	light green
bromine	+59	liquid	deep orange (reddish-brown)
iodine	+187	solid	dark grey

Exam tip

When predicting a property of a halogen, first look at your Periodic Table to see where it is in the Group, then look to see which way the trend in this property is going.

How science works

Elements with very high atomic numbers can only be made in atomic reactors. Some scientists think that it may be possible to make a halogen below astatine in the Periodic Table.

Suggest why this element has not yet been made.

Test yourself

1 Why is there no reaction between sodium bromide and iodine?

2 Both chlorine and bromine react with sodium. Which one reacts most vigorously?

3 Write a balanced symbol equation for the reaction of iodine with potassium.

4 Look at the table above showing the boiling point, state and colour of the halogens. Astatine is below iodine in Group 7. Predict the boiling point, state and colour of astatine.

5 Write a balanced symbol equation for the reaction of chlorine with sodium iodide.

C3f Electrolysis

After revising this item you should:

- be able to explain what happens during the electrolysis of dilute sulfuric acid and how electrolysis is used in the extraction of aluminium.

Dilute sulfuric acid electrolysis

Sulfuric acid is broken down by electrolysis into hydrogen and oxygen.

- Hydrogen bubbles off at the cathode.
- Oxygen bubbles off at the anode.

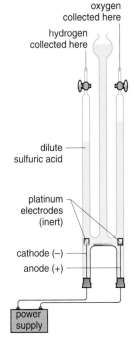

Electrode reactions

The ions present in sulfuric acid are OH^-, H^+ and SO_4^{2-}. During electrolysis the hydrogen ions move towards the cathode because it is negatively charged. They take up electrons from the cathode and become hydrogen atoms. These join up to form molecules of hydrogen gas.

$$2H^+ + 2e^- \rightarrow H_2$$

The hydroxide ions (which come from the water) and the sulfate ions move towards the anode because it is positively charged. The hydroxide ions give up their electrons to the anode and form molecules of oxygen gas.

$$4OH^- \rightarrow 2H_2O + O_2 + 4e^-$$

The sulfate ions remain in solution because they do not give off electrons as easily as hydroxide ions.

Extracting aluminium

Reactive metals such as aluminium are found in the rocks as minerals. The aluminium is present in the bauxite ore as the compound aluminium oxide.

We can purify the bauxite and use the pure molten aluminium oxide as the electrolyte in an electrolysis cell. The anodes and cathode in this cell are made of a type of carbon called **graphite**.

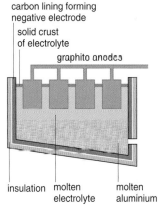

An electrolysis cell used in the manufacture of aluminium.

This electrolysis needs a large amount of electrical energy to work. A large electric current is passed through molten aluminium oxide. This keeps the aluminium oxide molten as well as decomposing it into aluminium and oxygen. The equation for this is:

$2Al_2O_3$	$\rightarrow$	$4Al$	+	$3O_2$
aluminium oxide	$\rightarrow$	aluminium	+	oxygen

Aluminium is expensive to produce because the process uses a large amount of electricity. Cryolite is added to the aluminium oxide to lower its melting point, which helps to reduce the amount of electricity used.

Electrode reactions in electrolysis

The ions present in molten aluminium oxide are Al^{3+} and O^{2-}. During electrolysis aluminium ions move towards the cathode. Here, they take up electrons from the cathode and become aluminium atoms.

$$Al^{3+} + 3e^- \longrightarrow Al$$

The oxide ions move towards the anode. Here, they give up their electrons to the anode and form oxygen atoms. These join together to form molecules of oxygen gas.

$$2O^{2-} - 4e^- \longrightarrow O_2$$

The oxygen reacts with the hot graphite anodes. The anodes get smaller and smaller because they are oxidised to carbon dioxide gas which escapes into the air.

This means that the anodes have to be replaced frequently.

Test yourself

1 Aluminium oxide is an ionic compound. Why does aluminium oxide need to be molten for it to be electrolysed?

2 The overall equation for the electrolysis of sulfuric acid is $2H_2O \longrightarrow 2H_2 + O_2$.

  What does this equation tell you about the number of hydrogen molecules formed compared with the number of oxygen molecules?

3 Aluminium is extracted from an electrolyte mixture of cryolite and aluminium oxide at about 1000°C. It is theoretically possible to extract aluminium by heating aluminium oxide with carbon at temperatures above 2500°C. Suggest why this is not done.

4 Is the following electrode reaction oxidation or reduction? Explain your answer.
$$2O^{2-} - 4e^- \longrightarrow O_2$$

C3g Transition elements & C3h Metal structure and properties

After revising these items you should:

● be able to describe how metallic bonding explains the properties of metals and describe some properties of transition elements and their compounds.

Transition elements and their compounds

The **transition elements** are metals which are found together in a block in the middle of the Periodic Table.

Transition elements and their compounds are often catalysts. For example:

• iron in the Haber Process
• nickel in the manufacture of margarine.

Unlike other metal compounds, **transition metal** compounds are usually coloured.

• Copper compounds are blue.
• Iron(II) compounds are light green.
• Iron(III) compounds are orange or brown.

Breaking down transition metal carbonates

Thermal decomposition is a reaction in which a compound is broken down into at least two other substances by heat. When transition metal carbonates are decomposed by heat a metal oxide (solid) and carbon dioxide (gas) are formed. The metal oxide is usually a different colour from the metal carbonate.

$CuCO_3$	$\rightarrow$	CuO	$+$	CO_2
copper(II) carbonate	$\rightarrow$	copper(II) oxide	$+$	carbon dioxide

Exam tip

You only have to learn one symbol equation for the thermal decomposition of transition metal carbonates because they are exactly the same, except for the symbol of the metal.

Identifying ions

We can test for many ions by **precipitation** reactions. These reactions occur when two solutions react to form an insoluble solid (the **precipitate**). When sodium hydroxide solution is added to a solution of a transition element compound a precipitate is formed.

The colour of this precipitate can be used to identify the transition metal ion in solution.

- Copper(II) ions, Cu^{2+}, give a blue precipitate.
- Iron(II) ions, Fe^{2+}, give a grey-green precipitate.
- Iron(III) ions, Fe^{3+}, give an orange-brown precipitate.

We can write ionic equations for the reactions between sodium hydroxide and copper(II), iron(II) and iron(III) ions. They follow a similar pattern. One hydroxide ion is needed for each positive charge on the metal ion.

Cu^{2+}	$+$	$2OH^-$	$\rightarrow$	$Cu(OH)_2$
copper(II) ion	$+$	hydroxide ion	$\rightarrow$	copper hydroxide

Fe^{3+}	$+$	$3OH^-$	$\rightarrow$	$Fe(OH)_3$
iron(III) ion	$+$	hydroxide ion	$\rightarrow$	iron(III) hydroxide

Exam tip

Make a list of all the tests for gases and ions you come across (e.g. carbon dioxide and copper(II) ions). Test yourself on these regularly by using flash cards or getting someone else to test you.

Metallic bonds

The particles in a metal are held close together by **metallic bonding**, in which a lattice of positive metal ions is held together by a 'sea' of electrons. These electrons are described as free, mobile or delocalised because they can move throughout the metal. There is a strong electrostatic attraction between the 'sea' of delocalised electrons and close packed positive metal ions.

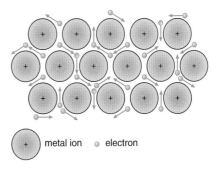

+ metal ion   ⊙ electron

Metallic bonding.

Exam tip

Remember that only some of the electrons in the metal structure are able to move. It is a common mistake to think that the lattice consists of atomic nuclei rather than positive ions and that all the electrons move.

Explaining the properties of metals

Metallic bonding is responsible for giving metals many of their typical properties:

- High melting and boiling points – due to strong forces of attraction between the delocalised electrons and the positive metal ions (cations). It takes a lot of energy to overcome these forces of attraction.
- Good electricity conduction – because the delocalised electrons are free to move past the regular arrangement of metal cations when the metal is connected to a power supply.

We can explain why some metals are suited to a particular use using this model. For example:

- metals which have higher tensile strength must have stronger forces of attraction between the metal cations and the delocalised electrons
- metals which are better conductors must have electrons which move more easily.

Exam tip

You will be expected to explain why metals are suited for particular uses. To do this you will also need to remember the typical properties of metals.

How science works

Safraz and Peter investigate the strength of pieces of a metal wire. They add weights to the wire until it breaks. Safraz adds 2 kg masses at a time and Peter adds 1 kg masses.

The table shows their results using a constant length of wire.

	Safraz			Peter				
	1st run	2nd run	3rd run	1st run	2nd run	3rd run	4th run	5th run
diameter of wire X (mm)	0.8	0.8	0.7	0.7	0.8	0.8	0.8	0.7
breaking mass (kg)	98	94	86	89	95	93	94	86

Comment on the validity and reliability of both sets of results.

Superconductors

Most substances have some resistance to the flow of electricity through them, but some materials can conduct electricity with little or no resistance. These are called **superconductors**.

Superconductors are used to:

- make powerful electromagnets
- make superfast electronic circuits
- transmit power with minimum energy loss.

The problem with many superconductors is that they only work at extremely low temperatures. That is why scientists are interested in developing superconductors which can work at 20°C.

How science works

Superconductors can transmit power with minimum energy loss, but they work only at very low temperatures. In recent years superconductors have been developed which work at slightly higher temperatures but not at normal air temperature.

An electricity company which is losing money because of power losses wants to invest into research into superconductors. Is this a sensible thing to do?

Test yourself

1. Compound X decomposes to form an oxide and carbon dioxide. The oxide reacts with an acid to form a solution which gives a grey-green precipitate, when sodium hydroxide is added. State the name of compound X.

2. Write an ionic equation for the reaction of iron(II) ions with sodium hydroxide ions.

3. State two ways in which metallic bonding differs from ionic bonding.

4. Titanium is stronger than magnesium. Use ideas about metallic bonding to explain this difference.

5. The information in the table compares the properties of three metals.

Metal	Melting point (°C)	Density (g/cm^3)	Electrical conductivity	Tensile strength
copper	1083	8.92	very good	medium
lead	328	11.34	good	low
iron	1535	7.87	good	very high

(a) Explain why copper is the best of these metals to use for electrical wiring.
(b) Explain why iron is the best of these metals for making a car body.

C4a Acids and bases

After revising this item you should:

- understand how acids are neutralised by bases and carbonates and know about salt formation during neutralisation, with equations

The pH scale

The **pH** scale shows how strongly acidic or alkaline a substance is. The pH value of a solution can be measured using universal indicator paper or solution. The colour of the universal indicator changes according to the pH value.

You can also find the pH value using a pH meter or a pH probe connected to a datalogger.

	pH
	1
strongly acidic	2
	3
	4
weakly acidic	5
	6
neutral	7
weakly alkaline	8
	9
	10
	11
strongly alkaline	12
	13
	14

Acids, alkalis and bases

The common laboratory acids are:

- hydrochloric acid
- sulfuric acid
- nitric acid.

All acids in solution in water contain hydrogen ions, H^+.

A **base** is a substance which neutralises an acid. Bases are often solids.

Examples of bases are:

- metal oxides, such as magnesium oxide
- metal hydroxides.

A base which dissolves in water is called an **alkali**. Many hydroxides, e.g. sodium hydroxide and calcium hydroxide, are alkalis.

All alkalis in solution in water contain hydroxide ions, OH^-.

Neutralisation

The equation for a **neutralisation** reaction is:

$$\text{acid} + \text{base} \longrightarrow \text{salt} + \text{water}$$

Water and most salt solutions are neutral. When a base reacts with an acid, the pH of the solution rises until there is no acid left. At this point the alkali has exactly reacted with the acid and you are left with only salt and water. The solution is neutral.

We can describe the neutralisation of an acid with an alkali by an ionic equation:

$$H^+ + OH^- \longrightarrow H_2O$$

When metal oxide and hydroxides neutralise acids they form salts. The name of the salt formed comes partly from the metal and partly from the acid. For example:

- hydrochloric acid forms metal chlorides
- nitric acid forms metal nitrates
- sulfuric acid forms metal sulfates.

Equations for acid–base reactions

Metal oxides and hydroxides react with acids to form a salt and water:

$$\underset{\substack{\text{sulfuric} \\ \text{acid}}}{H_2SO_4} + \underset{\substack{\text{copper(II)} \\ \text{oxide}}}{CuO} \longrightarrow \underset{\substack{\text{copper(II)} \\ \text{sulfate}}}{CuSO_4} + \underset{\text{water}}{H_2O}$$

$$\underset{\substack{\text{sulfuric} \\ \text{acid}}}{H_2SO_4} + \underset{\substack{\text{sodium} \\ \text{hydroxide}}}{2NaOH} \longrightarrow \underset{\substack{\text{sodium} \\ \text{sulfate}}}{Na_2SO_4} + \underset{\text{water}}{2H_2O}$$

$$\underset{\substack{\text{nitric} \\ \text{acid}}}{HNO_3} + \underset{\substack{\text{ammonia} \\ \text{solution}}}{NH_3} \longrightarrow \underset{\substack{\text{ammonium} \\ \text{nitrate}}}{NH_4NO_3}$$

Exam tip

Make sure that you can write the equations for the reactions of the three main acids with ammonia and metal hydroxides. Note that with ammonia there is no water on the right of the equation.

Metal carbonates neutralise acids to form a salt, water and carbon dioxide.

$$Na_2CO_3 + 2HCl \longrightarrow 2NaCl + H_2O + CO_2$$

sodium carbonate + hydro-chloric acid $\longrightarrow$ sodium chloride + water + carbon dioxide

Test yourself

1 Name the salts formed when:

(a) calcium carbonate reacts with nitric acid
(b) copper oxide reacts with sulfuric acid.

2 Describe how and explain why the pH changes when a solution of hydrochloric acid is gradually added to a solution of sodium hydroxide.

3 Write the simplest ionic equation for the reaction between hydrochloric acid and sodium hydroxide.

4 Write a balanced equation for the reaction between calcium carbonate and nitric acid.

5 Write a balanced equation for the reaction of ammonia with sulfuric acid.

C4b Reacting masses & C4c Fertilisers and crop yield

After revising these items you should:

● understand why mass is conserved, know how to work out masses of reactants, products and percentage yield in a reaction and understand the reasons for using fertilisers and some problems caused by their use.

Relative atomic mass and relative formula mass

Relative formula mass (M_r) is found by adding together the **relative atomic masses** (A_r) of each atom.

Here are some examples:

A_r	Working out M_r
Na = 23, Br = 80	NaBr = 23 + 80 = M_r of 103
Mg = 24, Cl = 35.5	$MgCl_2$ = 24 + (2 × 35.5) = M_r of 95

Using brackets in formulae

Sometimes, particular atoms are paired together, e.g. OH and SO_4. You should learn to recognise these groups.

If there is more than one of these groups in a compound, they are bracketed, e.g. $Fe(OH)_2$. The 2 here multiplies whatever is in the brackets. So the M_r of this compound is worked out like this:

A_r: Fe = 56, O = 16, H = 1
$Fe(OH)_2$ has one Fe, two Os and two Hs.
So the M_r is 56 + 2 × (16 + 1) = 90.

Exam tip

If the formula has a group in brackets, it is easier to work out the formula mass inside the brackets first, then multiply by the number outside the brackets.

Masses of reactants and products

When a reaction takes place, the atoms rearrange to form the new products. No atoms are gained or lost, so the total mass of the reactants is the same as the total mass of the products. We say that the mass is conserved.

$$2Mg + O_2 \longrightarrow 2MgO$$

reactants   product

In this equation:

• there are two atoms of magnesium and two atoms of oxygen in the reactants

• there is the same number of atoms in the product.

Exam tip

Remember that a number in front of a formula multiplies all the way through the formula.

Calculating masses of reactants or products

If we use a greater mass of reactants we get a greater mass of products. This is true as long as the mass of all the reactants is greater.

You can use simple maths to calculate the mass of the product obtained from a given amount of reactant. For example:

> When 48 g of magnesium react with 32 g of oxygen, 80 g of magnesium oxide is made.
>
> How many grams of magnesium oxide can be made from 12 g of magnesium?
>
> 48 g of magnesium give 80 g of magnesium oxide, so 12 g of magnesium make $(12 \div 48) \times 80 = 20$ g of magnesium oxide.

Even if you are not told the amounts of reactants and products you can still work out the amount of product from a given mass of reactant. You will need to know the equation. First work out the relative formula masses, then multiply these by the numbers in front of the formulae. For example:

> Calculate the mass of water formed when 4 g of methane (CH_4) are burned. (C = 12, H = 4, O = 16)
>
> $$CH_4 \quad + \quad 2O_2 \quad \rightarrow \quad CO_2 \quad + \quad 2H_2O$$
> $12 + (4 \times 1)$ gives $2 \times (2 + 16)$
>
> 16 g of methane   gives   36 g of water
>
> So 4 g of methane   gives $\dfrac{4 \times 36}{16} = 9$ g of water

Exam tip

Always show your working in calculations. Put the relevant numbers below each compound in the equation so that you can clearly see which figures to use.

Yield

We can calculate the amount of product that we expect to get from the reactants. This is called the **predicted yield**. The amount of product we actually get by experiment is called the **actual yield**.

Chemists often use **percentage yield** as a way of comparing the amount of product made with amount expected.

We can calculate percentage yield by using the formula:

$$\text{percentage yield} = \frac{\text{actual yield}}{\text{predicted yield}} \times 100$$

> A scientist calculates that 80 g of magnesium oxide should be formed when magnesium reacts with excess oxygen. An experiment shows that 48 g of magnesium oxide is formed.
>
> The percentage yield is:
>
> $$\frac{48}{80} \times 100 = 60\%$$

How science works

Kate prepared a sample of nickel sulfate by adding a calculated amount of sulfuric acid to a known amount of nickel carbonate. She heated the mixture for 10 minutes and then filtered it. The filtrate was left in the open air and allowed to crystallise.

The yield of crystals was much lower than expected. Suggest why.

What are fertilisers?

Fertilisers:

- increase the crop yield by replacing the **essential elements** (nitrogen, phosphorus and potassium) taken from the soil by crop plants
- provide extra amounts of nitrogen so that more of this element gets into plant proteins and increases crop growth
- are soluble in water so they are absorbed by plant roots.

How science works

When mixed with other chemicals, fertilisers can be explosive. Fertilisers are readily available from garden centres and farmers store large quantities of them.

Some people think that the Government should pass laws to make the sale of fertilisers more difficult. Give arguments for and against this suggestion.

Eutrophication

Eutrophication is the process by which lakes and rivers become 'dead' through pollution by fertilisers.

The diagram shows the process.

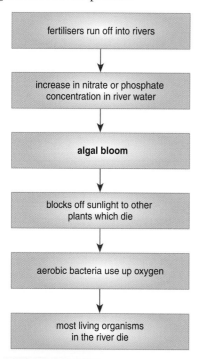

You can do a similar calculation for other elements present in a compound.

Exam tip

Make sure that you know how to calculate the relative formula mass of fertilisers such as ammonium nitrate (NH_4NO_3) and ammonium sulfate (($NH_4)_2SO_4$) (see page 40).

Making fertilisers

Fertilisers are salts made by neutralising particular acids with particular alkalis.

Alkali used	Acid used	Fertiliser made
ammonia	nitric acid	ammonium nitrate
ammonia	phosphoric acid	ammonium phosphate
ammonia	sulfuric acid	ammonium sulfate
potassium hydroxide	nitric acid	potassium nitrate

We can make a fertiliser using a titration procedure:

1   Put acid into a flask using an accurate pipette or measuring cylinder.

2   Fill a burette with alkali.

3   Put a few drops of an indicator into the flask.

4   Add alkali from the burette until the indicator in the flask just changes colour.

5   Repeat the process without the indicator, adding the correct volume of alkali.

6   Evaporate off some of the water then leave to crystallise.

7   Separate off the crystals by **filtration**, then wash and dry them.

Exam tip

You should know the names of the acids and alkalis used to make particular fertilisers and realise that the indicator colour changes when the solution is neutral.

How science works

Organic wastes from farms such as manure, silage and vegetable washings are high in nitrogen and phosphorus. What should farmers do to make sure that these wastes do not cause eutrophication?

Calculating percentage mass

We can find the percentage of nitrogen in a fertiliser using the formula:

$$\frac{\text{total mass of nitrogen in fertiliser}}{\text{relative formula mass of fertiliser}} \times 100$$

So to find the percentage of nitrogen in ammonium nitrate (NH_4NO_3) using the atomic masses H = 1, N = 14, O = 16:

two nitrogen atoms	$\rightarrow$	2×14

$$= 35\%$$

M_r of ammonium nitrate	$\rightarrow$	$(2 \times 14) + (4 \times 1) + (3 \times 16)$

Look at the Periodic Table to find relative atomic masses.

1 Calculate the relative formula mass of:

  (a) ammonium sulfate $(NH_4)_2SO_4$

  (b) urea $(NH_2)_2CO$

2 When 8 g of sulfur burns in excess oxygen, 16 g of sulfur dioxide is formed. What mass of sulfur dioxide is formed when 40 g of sulfur is burned?

3 Amelia heated 10 g of calcium carbonate. It decomposed to form 5.6 g of calcium oxide. The only other substance formed was carbon dioxide which was given off as a gas. What mass of carbon dioxide was formed?

4 Calculate the mass of copper(II) sulfate formed when 10 g of copper oxide reacts with excess sulfuric acid. The equation is:

  $CuO + H_2SO_4 \longrightarrow CuSO_4 + H_2O$

5 Oliver reacted 56 g of iron powder with excess sulfuric acid. The predicted yield of iron(II) sulfate was 152 g. After crystallisation, Oliver obtained 136.8 g of iron(II) sulfate. Calculate the percentage yield.

6 Describe how you could prepare a pure dry sample of potassium nitrate using a titration method.

7 State the name of the acids and alkalis needed to prepare:

  (a) ammonium nitrate
  (b) ammonium phosphate.

8 Calculate the percentage of potassium in the fertiliser potassium nitrate KNO_3.

C4d Making ammonia & C4f Batch or continuous?

After revising these items you should:

- understand how ammonia is made by the Haber Process and the conditions used, give some uses of ammonia and understand about batch and continuous processes, speciality and bulk chemicals and development and production costs.

The Haber Process

Ammonia is produced in great quantities to make fertilisers. Fertilisers are put on the soil to increase crop growth so that enough food can be produced for the ever expanding world population.

Ammonia is made from nitrogen and hydrogen. The reaction is a **reversible reaction** – it can go in either direction.

$$N_2 \quad + \quad 3H_2 \quad \rightleftharpoons \quad 2NH_3$$
$$\text{nitrogen} \; + \; \text{hydrogen} \; \rightleftharpoons \; \text{ammonia}$$

The nitrogen comes from the air. The hydrogen comes from natural gas or the cracking of oil fractions.

Conditions used:

- high pressure
- temperature of 450°C
- the presence of an iron catalyst.

High pressure increases the percentage yield of ammonia because it pushes the hydrogen and nitrogen molecules together.

The increase in temperature has two effects:

- It increases the rate of reaction.
- It lowers the percentage yield of ammonia.

A 'compromise' temperature of 450°C is chosen to give a fast reaction with a sufficiently high yield of ammonia.

Some important points:

- Nitrogen and hydrogen combine in a reactor vessel packed with the iron catalyst.
- The iron catalyst increases the rate of reaction but does not change the percentage yield of ammonia.
- Not all the nitrogen and hydrogen combine to make ammonia.
- Unreacted nitrogen and hydrogen are recycled so they are not wasted.
- Ammonia is made all the time as more hydrogen and nitrogen go into the reactor, and is continuously removed as a liquid. This type of process is called a **continuous process**.

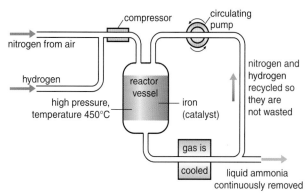

The Haber process.

> **Exam tip**
>
> *You must be able to interpret data in tables or graphs which show percentage yields in reversible reactions.*

The cost of making a substance

The total cost of making a product like ammonia depends on the cost of these factors:

gas or electricity which supplies the energy	higher temperature and pressure means greater energy cost
starting material	costs can be reduced by recycling unreacted materials
labour (wages)	using computer **automation** reduces costs as fewer workers are needed to operate the chemical process
chemical equipment (chemical plant)	carrying out the process under pressure needs special plant, which is expensive
catalysts	the rate of reaction must be high enough to give a good daily yield of product – catalysts help reduce the cost by speeding up the reaction

The conditions used in making a chemical must give the highest possible daily yield of product which is economical.

This means that the optimum (best) conditions are those which give the lowest cost (rather than the fastest reaction or the highest percentage yield). A low yield is acceptable if the reaction is repeated many times and the starting materials are recycled.

Making speciality chemicals

Chemicals such as medicines and **pharmaceutical drugs** are often made by a **batch process**. This means that they are made in small quantities as and when they are needed.

These speciality chemicals are made on a small scale compared with bulk chemicals such as ammonia which require a large-scale continuous process.

> **Exam tip**
>
> *You must be prepared to answer questions comparing batch and continuous processes when given relevant data and information.*

The raw materials for producing speciality chemicals are made:

- synthetically (from other laboratory chemicals), or

- from chemicals extracted from plants.

We can extract chemicals from plants by:

1   Crushing the plant.

2   Dissolving the crushed material in a suitable solvent.

3   Using **chromatography** to separate the required chemical.

The cost of developing a new substance

Development of a new medicine or pharmaceutical drug is expensive. The product may be on the market for many years before it pays for the cost of its own development. The spider diagram shows the costs involved.

Test yourself

1. A rare acid is found in some trees in India. Only one company in the world supplies it. A standard bottle of this chemical contains 5 g. A scientist wants to use this acid for her research. Why is this acid so expensive for her to buy? Give at least two reasons.

2. Why are pharmaceutical drugs tested on animals before they are tested on human volunteers?

3. Explain why the synthesis of ammonia is not carried out:

   (a) at temperatures much greater than 450°C
   (b) at temperatures much less than 450°C.

4. The table shows the monthly demand in kilograms for two chemicals, A and B.

Month	Jan	Feb	Mar	Apr	May	Jun	Jul
A	500	50	1050	24	10	150	250
B	55 000	60 000	65 000	55 000	70 000	75 000	55 000

   (a) What is the advantage of making chemical A by a batch process?
   (b) What is the disadvantage of making chemical B by a batch process?

5. The table shows the yield of ammonia in the Haber Process when different pressures are used in the reaction vessel. The temperature is kept the same.

percentage yield (%)	12	22	38	50	55	59
pressure (atmospheres)	50	100	200	300	400	500

   (a) Using this information estimate the percentage yield obtained when the pressure is 75 atmospheres and 600 atmospheres.
   (b) The chief chemist suggests that the process is carried out at a pressure of no more than 200 atmospheres. What are his reasons for this?

C4e Detergents

After revising this item you should:

- understand how detergents clean and how dry-cleaning works.

What are detergents?

A **detergent** is a substance which cleans. Detergents include:

- washing powders
- washing-up liquids
- soaps.

Many detergents, especially soaps, are salts made by the neutralisation of acids with alkalis. Many synthetic detergents are made from chemicals in crude oil.

This simplified diagram of a detergent molecule shows that it has a charged end and an uncharged end.

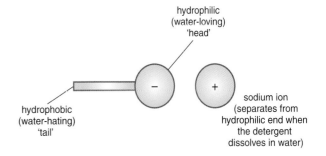

hydrophilic (water-loving) 'head'

hydrophobic (water-hating) 'tail'

sodium ion (separates from hydrophilic end when the detergent dissolves in water)

The charged 'head' end is water loving (hydrophilic), so it is attracted to water.

The uncharged 'tail' end is water hating (hydrophobic), so it is attracted to oil and grease.

How do detergents clean?

When clothes are washed:

1   The grease-loving 'tails' of the detergent molecules are attracted to the greasy dirt.

2   The detergent 'tails' stick into the grease.

3   The 'heads' are attracted to the water molecules.

4   The attraction between the 'heads' and the water molecules causes the grease to gradually roll up into a ball.

5   As this happens, the grease is pulled off the clothes.

6   The balls of grease are kept suspended in the water so that they do not go back onto the clothes.

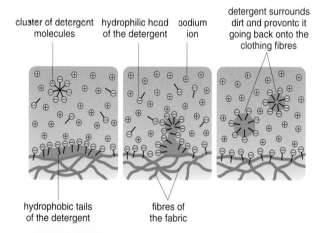

cluster of detergent molecules hydrophilic head of the detergent sodium ion detergent surrounds dirt and prevents it going back onto the clothing fibres

hydrophobic tails of the detergent   fibres of the fabric

> ### Exam tip
>
> *Make sure that you know the meaning of chemical terms such as solute, solution, solvent, soluble, insoluble, hydrophilic and hydrophobic.*

The best way to wash clothes

The advantages of washing clothes at a low temperature with the correct powder are:

- less energy used
- less shrinkage caused
- less likely to damage clothes made from silk or wool.

Enzymes are biological catalysts used in low temperature washes to remove food stains. They do not work well at temperatures above 40°C.

Water molecules have small positive and negative charges. They attract and dissolve other substances which are charged. They do not attract molecules like grease molecules which have no charge.

Some clothes cannot be washed in water because they may shrink or they are dyed with colours which wash out easily. These clothes have to be dry-cleaned.

Dry-cleaning

The spider diagram shows why **dry-cleaning** is useful.

uses organic solvent

does not use water

clothes do not shrink

dry-cleaning solvent

removes fatty stains

does not wash out water soluble dyes

Dry-cleaning works like this:

1   There are intermolecular forces of attraction between the grease molecules and the dry-cleaning solvent molecules.

2   These forces make the grease molecules dissolve in the dry-cleaning solvent.

3   The solution of grease is removed leaving some solvent on the clothes. This solvent evaporates off the clothes.

4   The clothes are left clean.

> ### Exam tip
>
> *In the exam you may be asked to comment on data from experiments which compare how well different washing powders and dry-cleaning solvents remove dirt and stains.*

How science works

Juan wants to compare how well grease dissolves in four different solvents. The solvents all evaporate readily and some are poisonous.

Suggest how he could carry out the experiment to make it a fair test.

Test yourself

1 Gordon has a shirt that has been stained with food. He washes the shirt at 60°C with a washing powder containing enzymes. Not all the stain is removed. Why is this?

2 What are the advantages of washing clothes at a low temperature?

3 Five equally stained pieces of cotton were washed under different conditions. The results are shown in the table. Suggest reasons for the differences in stain removal.

Treatment	Soap at 30°C	Soap at 60°C	Enzyme washing powder at 30°C	Dry-cleaning solvent
Dirt removed (%)	45	55	75	90

4 Which of the following will dissolve grease?

   A   Dry-cleaning solvent.
   B   Water.
   C   Salt solution.

   Give reasons for your answer.

5 State two advantages of dry-cleaning over cleaning with a detergent.

C4g Nanochemistry

After revising this item you should:

● be able to describe the three forms of carbon, their properties and uses and understand the concept of nanochemistry.

Diamond and graphite – structure and properties

Different forms of the same element are called **allotropes**. There are three allotropes of carbon:

● diamond
● graphite
● buckminsterfullerene

The diagrams shows the structures of the first two.

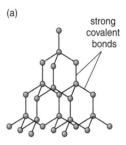

(a)   strong covalent bonds

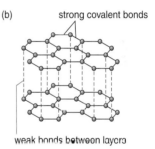

(b)   strong covalent bonds

weak bonds between layers

The arrangement of carbon atoms in (a) diamond (b) graphite.

Properties of graphite:

● black solid with a layered structure
● strong covalent bonding within the layers
● weak forces between the layers
● high melting point due to the presence of many strong covalent bonds which need to be broken
● slippery because the layers can slide over each other due to the weak forces between them.

Not all of the electrons in graphite are involved in bonding the carbon atoms covalently. Some are free to move along the layers.

These electrons are called **delocalised** electrons (see page 37). Graphite conducts electricity because these delocalised electrons can move when a voltage is applied.

Properties of diamond:

- lustrous, colourless solid
- very hard
- high melting point
- does not conduct electricity because it has no delocalised electrons to move.

The hardness and high melting point of diamond is due to the presence of many strong covalent bonds. These cannot be broken unless the temperature is extremely high.

Exam tip

You must be able to link the properties of diamond and graphite to their structures. List the properties and structure of each one in two columns, then cover up one list and test yourself.

Buckminsterfullerene

Buckminsterfullerene is a molecule which has 60 carbon atoms arranged like a football. Its formula is C_{60}.

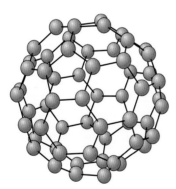

Fullerenes can be used as cages to trap other molecules. One idea is to trap drug molecules inside the cage or attach drugs to the outside of the cage and use the fullerenes to deliver drugs to where they are needed in the body. This means there will be less damage to other cells in the body.

Exam tip

You must be able to spot similarities and differences between the three forms of carbon from diagrams showing their structure.

Nanotubes

Fullerenes can be joined together to make **nanotubes**. The cylindrical shape of nanotubes makes them very strong. Like graphite, they conduct electricity.

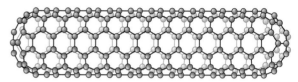

Nanotubes can be used as:
- semiconductors in electrical circuits
- industrial catalysts
- reinforcement for the graphite in tennis rackets.

When nanotubes are used as catalysts, groups of catalyst atoms are attached to the outer surface of the nanotube. A huge surface area is available for catalysis because they are so small.

Nanochemistry

Molecular manufacturing means making substances on a very small scale.

In recent years scientists have been able to move groups of atoms around on special surfaces and create materials, like nanotubes, at the atomic level. They build up the product a few atoms at a time, or atoms are removed from a larger structure a few at a time. We call this process of arranging atoms **positional chemistry**.

Chemists have found that **nanoparticles** have different properties from 'bulk' chemicals (chemicals used on a larger scale). Nanochemistry works on a very small scale compared to traditional chemistry, which uses 'bulk' chemicals on a large scale.

How science works

Nanoparticles are used in some sunblock creams and car bumpers. Fine soot also contains nanoparticles.

Research using rats has shown that nanoparticles can accumulate in the lungs. Many people are worried about these findings.

How should scientists respond to these worries?

C4h How pure is our water?

Water resources

In many developing nations clean water is a resource often in short supply. Lack of water destroys crops and kills animals. In these countries water may come from wells or ponds which are contaminated with microbes which cause disease.

Even in wetter countries it is important to conserve water because occasional droughts or overuse can lead to water shortages.

In some countries where there is little rain, seawater is distilled to make fresh water.

- This is expensive because it uses a lot of energy.
- The water produced has no taste because it has no dissolved salts.
- The water is free from contaminating materials.

How is water purified?

Before it is purified, water may contain:

- dissolved salts and minerals
- microbes
- insoluble materials such as animal remains and clay particles.

The diagram shows the stages in water purification.

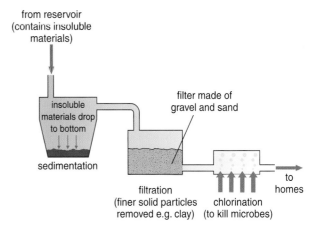

Water pollution

Pollutants are sometimes present in our purified water supply. They are difficult to remove during water purification because they are soluble in water.

They are generally present in such low concentrations that they are not harmful to health.

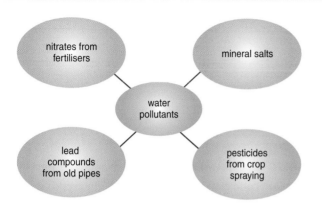

The word equations for the halide test all follow a similar pattern. Halides include:

- chlorides
- bromides
- iodides.

$$NaCl + AgNO_3 \rightarrow AgCl + NaNO_3$$
sodium chloride + silver nitrate → silver chloride + sodium nitrate
(white precipitate)

Some tests for ions

You can test for particular ions that may be present in water. These tests involve precipitation reactions (see page 37). You add a few drops of a colourless test solution to the water sample and observe the colour of the precipitate.

Ion tested for	Test solution added	Result if the ion is present
sulfate	barium chloride	white precipitate
chloride	silver nitrate	white precipitate
bromide	silver nitrate	cream precipitate
iodide	silver nitrate	pale yellow precipitate

The equation for the sulfate test is:

$$Na_2SO_4 + BaCl_2 \rightarrow BaSO_4 + 2NaCl$$
sodium sulfate + barium chloride → barium sulfate + sodium chloride
(white precipitate)

In this equation (and the one that follows) you can replace sodium with the name of another metal.

How science works

The table compares the amount of dissolved solids in the tap water in two towns. Nine samples were collected from different areas within each town.

Town	Amount of dissolved solids (mg/dm³)								
Addles	65.5	71.0	58.5	80.5	60.0	64.5	85.5	15.0	76.5
Becton	70	70	80	75	85	80	70	70	70

To what extent can these figures be used to compare the amount of dissolved solids in the two towns?

Test yourself

1 Explain why tap water is not pure water.

2 Drinking water often contains mineral salts which are not removed during water purification. Explain why this does not matter.

3 Why is it dangerous to drink unpurified water?

4 Write a symbol equation for the reaction of magnesium bromide solution with silver nitrate solution.

5 Anthea added a few drops of barium chloride solution to a sample of water. She observed that a white precipitate formed. Explain this observation with the aid of a symbol equation.

P3a Speed

After revising this item you should:

- be able to recall the relationship between speed, distance and time, calculate speeds, distances and times, and use distance–time graphs.

Calculating speed

Speed is measured in metres per second (m/s) or kilometres per hour (km/h).

Louise's car travels at a speed of 20 m/s. It will cover 20 metres in one second and 40 metres in two seconds.

At a faster speed of 30 m/s, she will cover a greater distance, 30 m, in each second and it will take less time to complete her journey.

To calculate speed you need to use this equation:

$$\text{speed} = \frac{\text{distance}}{\text{time}}$$

For example:

A cyclist travels 900 m in 1 minute. What is his speed in metres per second (m/s)?

distance = 900 m
time = 60 s
speed = ?

$$\text{speed} = \frac{900\,\text{m}}{60\,\text{s}}$$
$$= 15\,\text{m/s}$$

If you are given the speed and either the distance or time you need to rearrange the equation. The following diagram shows a triangle that can help you remember how to do this.

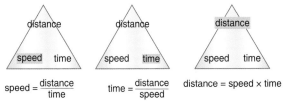

$$\text{speed} = \frac{\text{distance}}{\text{time}} \qquad \text{time} = \frac{\text{distance}}{\text{speed}} \qquad \text{distance} = \text{speed} \times \text{time}$$

Step 1. You are given 'speed = distance over time' so write the equation in the triangle. When you cover up speed, distance is 'over' time.

Step 2. To find time, cover time and you have 'distance over speed'.

For example:

A car travels at 80 km/h. How long will it take to go 280 km?

speed = 80 km/h
distance = 280 km
time = ?

$$\text{time} = \frac{\text{distance}}{\text{speed}}$$

$$\text{time} = \frac{280\,\text{km}}{80\,\text{km/h}}$$

$$= 3.5\,\text{h}$$

Exam tip

Always write down the rearranged equation you are using. You may get a mark for the equation but not the triangle.

Distance–time graphs

On a **distance–time graph**:

- a horizontal line means the object is stopped
- a sloping straight line means it has a steady speed
- a line curving upwards means the speed is increasing
- a line curving downwards means the speed is decreasing.

The steepness, or **gradient**, of the line shows the speed:

- A steeper gradient means a higher speed.

This graph is for a dog walking.

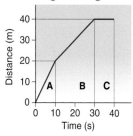

The following table shows the same information.

Section	Distance (m)	Time (s)	Speed (m/s)	Comment
A	20	10	2	
B	20	20	1	gradient not as steep as A, so speed is slower
C	0	10	0	stopped

One way the police measure the speed of cars is to have cables running under the road 10 cm apart. These detect the pressure of the car going over them.

The time between the car crossing the first and second cable is used to work out the speed. If the car is exceeding the speed limit a camera photographs the number plate.

Test yourself

1 In 2006 Asafa Powell held the 100 m world record with a time of 9.77 seconds. What was his speed?

2 If an athlete runs at a speed of 8 m/s how long will it take her to run 100 m?

3 Gareth drives his car at 50 km/h for 30 minutes, then at 80 km/h for 2 hours.

    (a) How far has he travelled?
    (b) Sketch a graph of the journey.

4 This graph shows different cycle rides.

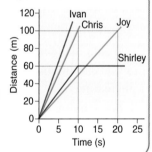

    (a) Which cyclist cycled fastest?
    (b) Which cyclist stopped cycling?
    (c) Work out the speed that Chris and Joy cycled.

P3b Changing speed

After revising this item you should:

- be able to describe, draw and interpret speed–time graphs, and to calculate acceleration, speed and time.

Speed–time graphs

The diagram shows a **speed–time graph** for an off-road journey by a motorbike.

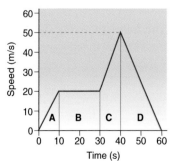

The gradient (steepness) of the graph is a measure of the acceleration. Part C is steeper than part A, so the acceleration is more in part C.

- In part A: the motorbike accelerates from 0 m/s to 20 m/s (a change of 20 m/s) in 10 s.
- In part C: the motorbike accelerates from 20 m/s to 50 m/s (a change of 30 m/s) in 10 s.

Exam tip

A common mistake is to confuse distance–time graphs with speed–time graphs.

Distance on a speed–time graph

The distance travelled is shown on a speed–time graph by the area under the graph.

In part B of the graph (between 10 s and 30 s) the motorbike has travelled at a constant speed of 20 m/s for 20 seconds. The distance travelled is the area of the rectangle.

part B	time	= 20 s (between 10 s and 30 s)
	speed	= 20 m/s
	distance travelled in B	= area of rectangle
		= 20 m/s × 20 s
		= 400 m
part A	the area of the triangle	= half of rectangle
		= 20 m/s × 10 s
	distance travelled in A	= area of triangle
		= ½ × 20 m/s × 10 s
		= 100 m
part C	The area is made of a triangle and a rectangle.

	area of triangle	=	½ × (50 − 20) m/s × (40 − 30) s
		=	½ × 30 m/s × 10 s
		=	150 m
	area of rectangle	=	20 m/s × 10 s
		=	200 m
	total distance travelled in part C	=	350 m
part D	the motorbike is decelerating (the gradient and acceleration are negative) the distance travelled is the area of the triangle		
	area of triangle	=	½ × 50 m/s × 20 s
		=	500 m

The total distance travelled in all four parts is:

$$\begin{array}{cccc} A & B & C & D \\ 100\,m + 400\,m + 350\,m + 500\,m = 1350\,m \end{array}$$

Acceleration on a speed–time graph

part A	accelerates from 0 m/s to 20 m/s (a change in speed of 20 m/s) in 10 s acceleration = 20 m/s ÷ 10 s = 2 m/s²
part B	no change in speed acceleration = 0 (constant speed)
part C	accelerates from 20 m/s to 50 m/s (a change in speed of 30 m/s) in 10 s acceleration = 30 m/s ÷ 10 s = 3 m/s²
part D	decelerates from 50 m/s to 0 m/s (a change in speed of −50 m/s) in 20 s acceleration = −50 m/s ÷ 20 s = −2.5 m/s²

Uniform and non-uniform acceleration

When the slope is a straight line the acceleration is constant. In part C it is $3\,m/s^2$ for the whole of the 10 seconds. In real life acceleration changes, and the graph is curved.

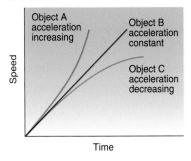

Calculating acceleration

Acceleration is the change in speed per unit time.

The unit of time is the second, so acceleration is change of speed per second. It is measured in metres per second squared (m/s^2).

$$acceleration \;=\; \frac{change\ in\ speed}{time\ taken}$$

For example:

1 Disney's *Rock 'n' Roller Coaster*® accelerates from 0 m/s to 27 m/s in 2.8 seconds. What is its acceleration in metres per second squared (m/s^2)?

$$\begin{aligned} change\ in\ speed &= 27\,m/s - 0\,m/s \\ &= 27\,m/s \\ time &= 2.8\,s \\ acceleration &= \frac{27\,m/s}{2.8\,s} \\ &= 9.64\,m/s^2 \end{aligned}$$

2 Acceleration due to gravity is $10\,m/s^2$. A stone falls and takes 4.4 seconds to hit the ground. What is its speed when it hits the ground?

$$\begin{aligned} change\ in\ speed &= acceleration \times time\ taken \\ &= 10\,m/s^2 \times 4.4\,s \\ &= 44\,m/s \end{aligned}$$

The stone started at 0 m/s so the final speed is 44 m/s.

change in speed

acceleration   time

Change in direction

An object is accelerating if it changes direction – even if its speed is constant.

A car cornering at constant speed and an object moving in a circle at constant speed are both accelerating.

A car's acceleration is given in the form '0 to 60 mph in 6 seconds'. The McLaren F1 supercar has an acceleration of 0 to 60 mph in 3.1 seconds (60 mph is 96 km/h).

$$
\text{change in speed} = 96\,000\,\text{m in 1 hour}
$$
$$
= \frac{96\,000}{60 \times 60}
$$
$$
= 26.67\,\text{m/s}
$$
$$
\text{acceleration} = \frac{26.67\,\text{m/s}}{3.1\,\text{s}}
$$
$$
= 8.6\,\text{m/s}^2
$$

Test yourself

1 This graph shows part of a horse ride.

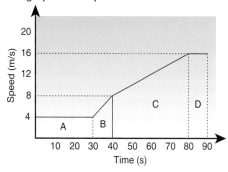

(a) What is the speed of the horse at the start of the graph?

(b) How many seconds after the start of the graph does the horse reach a speed of 16 m/s?

(c) In which part of the graph (A, B, C or D) does the horse have the greatest acceleration?

(d) What distance is travelled in part A?

(e) What is the acceleration in part B?

2 Sketch a speed–time graph for this journey:

A A motorcyclist accelerates from 0 m/s to 20 m/s in 5 seconds.

B She travels at this steady speed for 10 seconds.

C She accelerates to 30 m/s in 5 seconds.

D Finally she decelerates to 0 m/s in 20 seconds.

3 An aircraft accelerates from standstill on the runway at 1.2 m/s^2 for 75 seconds. What is its speed?

4 Which of these (A–E) have zero acceleration?

A Speeding up.

B Constant speed in a circle.

C Constant speed in a straight line.

D Stopped.

E Slowing down.

P3c Forces and motion & P3d Work and power

● be able to use the relationship between force, mass and acceleration, explain stopping distances and use the equations for work, energy and power.

Force, mass and acceleration

• For a given mass, increasing the force on it increases the acceleration.

• For a given force, increasing the mass reduces the acceleration.

> force (N) = mass (kg) × acceleration (m/s^2)

For example:

1 A Vampire dragster, a jet-powered car, has a mass of 1000 kg and accelerates at 20 m/s^2. Work out the accelerating force.

$$
\text{force} = 1000\,\text{kg} \times 20\,\text{m/s}^2
$$
$$
= 20\,000\,\text{N}
$$

2 A high-speed train has a mass of 750 000 kg and an accelerating force of 400 000 N. What is the acceleration?

$$
\text{acceleration} = \frac{\text{force}}{\text{mass}}
$$
$$
\text{acceleration} = \frac{400\,000\,\text{N}}{750\,000\,\text{kg}}
$$
$$
= 0.53\,\text{m/s}^2
$$

Forces

When a body A (an object) exerts a force on body B (another object), body B exerts an equal but opposite force on body A.

For example, when skateboarders, A and B, push each other:

• they both push with an equal but opposite force

• it is impossible for one to push with a larger force than the other

• they move apart with the same numerical value of acceleration if they have exactly the same mass, skateboard and ground surface.

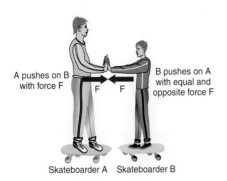

A pushes on B with force F

F F

B pushes on A with equal and opposite force F

Skateboarder A   Skateboarder B

All forces come in interaction pairs. From the point of view of body A we feel B pushing. But body B feels A pushing. They are different views of the same interaction.

When a skateboarder pushes a wall, the wall pushes back with an equal and opposite force. The skateboarder moves away from the wall.

The wall does not move because forces from the ground balance the force from the skateboarder. These are balanced forces on the wall.

Stopping distances

$$\text{stopping distance} = \text{thinking distance} + \text{braking distance}$$

This diagram shows the shortest stopping distances.

20 MPH	6 metres 6 metres	= 12 metres
40 MPH	12 metres 24 metres	= 36 metres
60 MPH	18 metres 55 metres	= 73 metres

Thinking distance
Braking distance

Driving safely includes:

- not driving too close to the car in front
- observing speed limits
- slowing down in poor road conditions.

Work done

Energy is transferred when **work** is done.

$$\text{work done (J)} = \text{force (N)} \times \text{distance (m)}$$

For example:

1 A man weighs 800 N. He climbs 10 m up a ladder. How much work has he done?
   work done = 800 N × 10 m = 8000 J

2 The braking force on a car is 6000 N. 576 000 J of work is done to stop the car. How far does it travel before it stops?

$$\text{distance} = \frac{\text{work done}}{\text{force}}$$

$$\text{distance} = \frac{576\,000\,\text{J}}{6000\,\text{N}}$$

$$= 96\,\text{m}$$

work done

force   distance

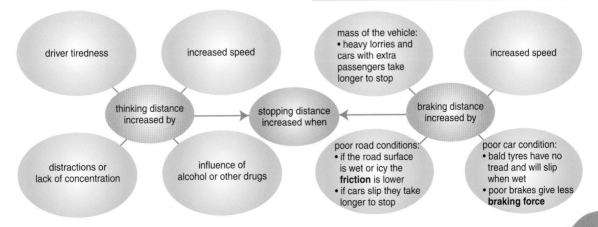

driver tiredness

increased speed

mass of the vehicle:
• heavy lorries and cars with extra passengers take longer to stop

increased speed

thinking distance increased by

stopping distance increased when

braking distance increased by

distractions or lack of concentration

influence of alcohol or other drugs

poor road conditions:
• if the road surface is wet or icy the **friction** is lower
• if cars slip they take longer to stop

poor car condition:
• bald tyres have no tread and will slip when wet
• poor brakes give less **braking force**

Power

$$\textbf{power } (W) = \frac{\text{work done (J)}}{\text{time (s)}}$$

For example:

1 A horse does 44 760 J of work pulling a cart for one minute. What power has it developed?

$$\text{power} = \frac{44\,760\,\text{J}}{60\,\text{s}}$$
$$= 746\,\text{W}$$

2 A 500 W pump is used to empty a pond. It does 600 kJ of work. How long did it take to empty the pond?

$$\text{time} = \frac{\text{work done}}{\text{power}}$$
$$\text{time} = \frac{600\,000\,\text{J}}{500\,\text{W}}$$
$$= 1200\,\text{s (or (20 minutes)}$$

work done
power   time

Fuel consumption

The following table compares cars with petrol engines. The power of the engine increases with engine capacity.

Vehicle	Engine capacity (cc or cm³)	CO$_2$ emitted (g/km)	Fuel consumption (litres/ 100 km)	Performance (mpg)
Vauxhall Corsa	998	115	4.8	58.8
Ford Focus	1596	180	7.5	37.7
Ford Galaxy	2792	288	12.0	23.5
Mitsubishi Shogun	3497	339	14.2	19.9
Lamborghini Diablo	5992	520	21.8	13.0

Source: Vehicle Certification Agency

Fuel consumption increases with engine power. Carbon dioxide emissions and other forms of pollution also increase.

Test yourself

1 (a) A car with mass 1400 kg accelerates at 5 m/s². What is the accelerating force?
   (b) A lorry with mass 3500 kg accelerates with a force of 7000 N. What is the acceleration?

2 A rowing boat drifts towards the bank of a lake. Explain, in terms of the forces on the bank and the boat, what happens when the rower pushes on the bank with an oar.

3 Use the chart of stopping distance (page 55) to compare:

   (a) the thinking distance, and
   (b) the braking distance

   at 20 mph and at 40 mph.

4 (a) Calculate the work done when a customer pushes a shopping trolley with a force of 8 N for a distance of 12 m.
   (b) 144 J of work is done pushing a second trolley 12 m. What is the pushing force?

5 An elephant does 48 000 J of work dragging a log for 75 s. The pulling force is 800 N.

   (a) How far does the elephant drag the log?
   (b) What power has the elephant developed?
   (c) How long would it take for a 800 W engine to do the same amount of work?

6 (a) Use the fuel consumption table opposite to explain how:
      (i) the emission of carbon dioxide is related to the power of the engine
      (ii) the fuel consumption changes as the power of the engine increases.
   (b) If petrol costs 90 p a litre how much does it cost to travel 100 km in:
      (i) the Mitsibushi Shogun
      (ii) the Vauxhall Corsa?

P3e Energy on the move & P3f Crumple zones

After revising these items you should:

- be able to work out kinetic energy, explain how it affects fuel consumption and braking distance, identify other factors that affect fuel consumption such as friction, driving speed and road conditions, and explain some safety features of modern cars.

Kinetic energy

All moving objects, e.g. vehicles, balls, animals and water, have **kinetic energy** (KE).

The kinetic energy is greater for objects with:

- higher speed
- greater mass (double the mass and you double the kinetic energy).

$$KE = \tfrac{1}{2} mv^2$$
where KE is kinetic energy (J)
m is mass (kg)
v is speed (v for velocity) (m/s).

Exam tip

You will be given this equation in the exam. Make sure you can use it. Do not forget to square the speed, or to multiply by a half. These are common mistakes.

For example:

What is the KE of a car of mass 1000 kg and speed 13 m/s?
$$KE = \tfrac{1}{2} \times 1000\,kg \times (13\,m/s)^2 = 84\,500\,J$$

Double the speed and the kinetic energy is four times as much, because it is squared.

For example:

What is the KE of the same car at 26 m/s?
$$KE = \tfrac{1}{2} \times 1000\,kg \times (26\,m/s)^2 = 338\,000\,J$$

Look at the braking distances in the shortest stopping distance chart on page 55:

- At 20 mph the braking distance is 6 m.
- At 40 mph the braking distance is 24 m.

When the speed of a car is doubled it has four times as much kinetic energy. At maximum braking force this means the braking distance is four times as far.

Fuel consumption

If a car is travelling at a steady speed it is still doing work against friction, so fuel is burned to supply the energy needed.

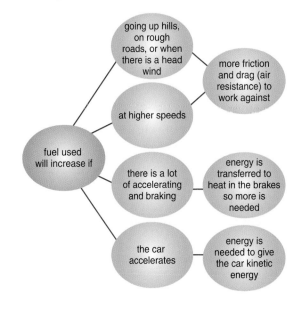

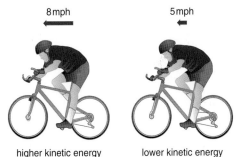

higher kinetic energy   lower kinetic energy

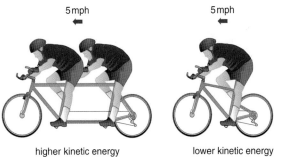

higher kinetic energy   lower kinetic energy

The following table shows fuel consumption for urban driving (stop-start city driving) and extra-urban driving (outside cities) for two different cars. The combined data is a cycle with some of both driving types. All cars have figures for these cycles which can be compared.

Car	Driving style	Fuel consumption (litres/100 km)	Performance (mpg)
Jaguar X-type	urban	7.7	36.6
	extra-urban	4.6	61.4
	combined	5.7	49.1
Renault Clio Campus	urban	7.4	38.2
	extra-urban	5.0	56.5
	combined	5.9	47.9

Source: Vehicle Certification Agency

Notice that the stop-start driving (urban cycle) uses more fuel. The Clio is intended for town driving. It has better consumption for this cycle than the Jaguar, but is not as good for the faster extra-urban driving.

Electric-powered cars

Fossil fuel (petrol, diesel and LPG) powered cars produce polluting gases including carbon dioxide.

Battery-powered cars:

- They do not give out exhaust gases so do not pollute at the point of use (on the roads).
- The batteries need recharging from an electricity supply.
- When this electricity is from a power station there is pollution produced at the power station.
- Batteries could be recharged from green sources such as solar or wind power.

Safety features

When a car stops, all the kinetic energy of the car, the driver, and the passengers must be safely transferred, e.g. to heat and sound. This is why brakes get very hot.

Allowing a long braking distance means that the braking force need not be so large. Escape lanes at the bottom of hills give extra distance for lorries to stop in an emergency.

It is the force, causing a large deceleration on the body, which causes injuries. We can reduce injuries by reducing the forces in a collision by:

- increasing the stopping or collision time
- increasing the stopping or collision distance
- decreasing acceleration (the acceleration in a collision is a deceleration, it needs to be kept as small as possible).

The following table show how forces are reduced in a collision.

Safety feature	Shape change	Absorb energy of	Increase collision time and distance	Driver and passengers decelerated more slowly
crumple zones	compressed	car	✓	✓
air bags	compressed	driver and passengers	✓	✓
seat belts	stretched	driver and passengers	✓	✓
crash barriers	compressed	car	✓	✓

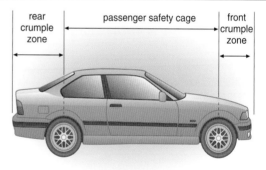

Active safety features

Here are some **active safety** features of a car.

anti-lock braking system (ABS)	• helps you stop without skidding • a car that skids takes much longer to stop • to stop in the shortest distance a car needs the maximum friction force possible without skidding • sensors measure the friction force, and if the wheel is about to skid the braking force is reduced slightly, automatically, so the car does not skid
traction control	increases or decreases the force on each wheel to increase the grip and stop the car skidding
safety cage	a strong frame that keeps its shape and protects the driver and passengers in a crash

Passive safety features

Here are some **passive safety** features of a car.

easily accessible controls so the driver does not lose control of the car	• electric windows can be opened at the touch of a button • stereo controls near the steering wheel • paddle shift controls for the gears are fitted to racing cars and a few modern cars – pressing a button (or paddle) on the steering wheel changes the gear without moving a lever or pressing the clutch
cruise control	keeps the car at a steady speed less tiring for the driver and makes it easier to stick to the speed limit
adjustable seating	improves visibility and comfort

Test yourself

1 Which has the greatest kinetic energy (A or B):

  (a) A a train travelling at 20 mph or B a lorry travelling at 20 mph

  (b) A a car travelling at 50 mph or B the same car travelling at 70 mph?

2 Calculate the kinetic energy of a car with a mass of 1200 kg and a speed of 26 m/s.

3 Look at the braking distances in the chart on page 55. Use these to estimate the braking distance for a car travelling at 80 mph.

4 Chloe says that battery-powered cars do not pollute. Eshan says they do. Explain how they could both be right.

5 Adam is wearing a seatbelt when his car is involved in a collision.

  (a) How does the seatbelt reduce the force on Adam?

  (b) Give another example of a car safety feature that reduces injury in a collision.

P3g Falling safely

After revising this item you should:

● be able to explain why falling objects increase speed and reach a terminal speed.

Falling

Objects falling through the Earth's atmosphere accelerate. As they get faster the frictional force from the air increases and this reduces their acceleration. If they do not hit the ground first, objects reach a steady speed called **terminal speed**.

Why objects increase in speed

A falling object accelerates because of its weight. This force, caused by gravity, pulls it towards the centre of the Earth.

In the atmosphere the air pushes upwards against a falling object. This frictional force is called air resistance or **drag**. The diagram shows these forces on a skydiver.

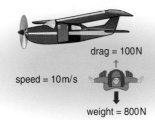

start of dive

drag = 100 N

speed = 10 m/s

weight = 800 N

Drag (or air resistance) increases as the object moves faster. Weight stays the same. As the object moves faster the downward force accelerating the object gets smaller because:

> downward force = weight – drag

The acceleration gets smaller but the speed is still increasing.

Why objects maintain a steady speed

The speed and drag increase until the forces are balanced.

> weight = drag

There is zero downward force and zero acceleration.

The falling object is now moving at a steady speed. It is not accelerating, so the drag stays the same. The object will not slow down or speed up because the forces are balanced. This steady speed is called the terminal speed.

The diagram shows the skydiver has reached terminal speed.

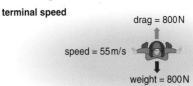

terminal speed

drag = 800 N

speed = 55 m/s

weight = 800 N

Using drag to decrease speed

Opening a parachute suddenly increases the drag because there is a large area for the air to push against. If the drag is larger than the weight the parachutist will slow down.

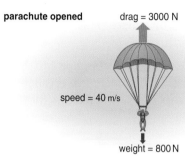

parachute opened   drag = 3000 N

speed = 40 m/s

weight = 800 N

drag = 800N

weight = 800N

The skydiver is slowing down and will eventually reach a new terminal speed as shown in the right-hand diagram.

The next diagram shows the speed–time graph for the whole jump.

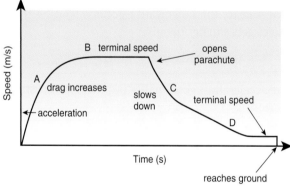

Speed (m/s)

A — drag increases

acceleration

B terminal speed

opens parachute

slows down

C

terminal speed

D

reaches ground

Time (s)

Free-fall

If the only force on a falling object is its weight, it is in **free-fall**. The acceleration is constant, because there are no other forces. On Earth or in orbit this force is called 'g' force.

A steel ball and a feather, inside a glass tube with no air, will fall with the same acceleration and hit the ground at the same time.

Test yourself

1   Describe what happens to the speed and the drag force on a falling ball

    (a)   before it falls   (b)   when it is first dropped
    (c)   if it continues to fall for several seconds.

2   Look at the speed–time graph of a skydiver during a parachute jump (opposite). Draw diagrams to show the forces on the skydiver at points A, B, C and D and explain what is happening at each point.

3   Which of these statements (A–F) are true?

    A   Falling objects increase speed when the drag is less than the weight.
    B   If drag is larger than weight, falling objects can move upwards.
    C   For objects at terminal speed, drag equals weight.
    D   When a parachute opens the drag force can be larger than the weight.
    E   The drag force depends on the speed of an object.
    F   The drag force depends on the weight of an object.

4   An astronaut on the Moon drops a hammer and a feather from a height of 3 m above the surface. Which of these statements (A–D) is true?

    A   The hammer weighs the same as the feather on the Moon.
    B   There are no drag forces because there is no atmosphere.
    C   The hammer and feather have no weight on the Moon.
    D   The hammer and the feather are both in free-fall.

5   Explain how a parachute braking system can be used to slow down a car.

P3h The energy of games and theme rides

After revising this item you should:

●   be able to calculate the gravitational potential energy of an object, explain that it can be converted to kinetic energy and back and explain how this is used in roller coasters, and be able to calculate the weight of an object.

Gravitational potential energy

- Water in a reservoir at the top of a hill has **gravitational potential energy** (PE). When the dam is opened the water flows downhill, gaining kinetic energy (KE). We can use this energy to turn the turbines of a hydroelectric power station.
- Alesha is on a trampoline. She goes up and slows down, losing KE and gaining the same amount of PE. At the top of the jump, for a moment, she is not moving. All the energy is PE. Then she starts to fall. The PE is converted back to KE so she gets faster and faster.
- As a skydiver falls he loses PE and gains KE until he reaches terminal speed. At terminal speed KE does not increase. There is a frictional force slowing the skydiver. The PE is used to do work against this force.

Gravitational field strength

On the Earth the **gravitational field strength** is six times greater than on the Moon.

The amount of PE an object gains by moving up on the Earth is six times greater than it would be if the object moved up the same distance on the Moon.

Potential energy is greater when the gravitational field strength is greater.

Calculating weight

On Earth all objects with mass are attracted downwards by gravity. We call the force on them weight.

Use this formula to find weight:

$$\text{weight (N)} = \text{mass (kg)} \times \text{gravitational field strength (N/kg)}$$

On the Earth, g = 10 N/kg.

Exam tip

You will always be given this value for g in the exam.

For example:

1. Sophie has a mass of 55 kg. What is her weight?

   W = 55 kg × 10 N/kg
   = 550 N

2. The weight of an airliner is 5 600 000 N. What is its mass?

   $$\text{Mass} = \frac{\text{weight}}{\text{gravitational field strength}}$$
   $$= \frac{5\,600\,000\,\text{N}}{10\,\text{N/kg}}$$
   $$= 560\,000\,\text{kg}$$

Calculating potential energy

$$\text{gravitational potential energy (J)} = \text{mass (kg)} \times \text{gravitational field strength (N/kg)} \times \text{height (m)}$$

$$\text{PE} = mgh$$

Exam tip

If you know the weight, you can calculate PE using

PE = weight × height change

For example:

Louise has a mass of 50 kg and climbs 60 m to the top of a monument. How much PE has she gained?

Using g = 10 N/kg
PE = 50 kg × 10 N/kg × 60 m
= 30 000 J

How high would she have to climb to gain 10 000 J?

$$h = \frac{\text{PE}}{mg}$$
$$= \frac{10\,000\,\text{J}}{50\,\text{kg} \times 10\,\text{N/kg}}$$
$$= 20\,\text{m}$$

Roller coaster rides

1 A motor is often used to move the car to the top of a slope – giving it PE.

2 The car then travels down the slope, gaining KE and losing PE.

3 The car goes up the next slope, losing KE and gaining PE.

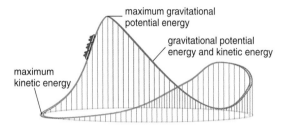

maximum gravitational potential energy

gravitational potential energy and kinetic energy

maximum kinetic energy

For example:

1 A roller coaster car with mass 2000 kg starts at the top of a 50 m slope. What is its speed at the bottom? (Use g = 10 N/kg.)

$$\text{PE lost} = mgh$$
$$= 2000\,\text{kg} \times 10\,\text{N/kg} \times 50\,\text{m}$$
$$= 1\,000\,000\,\text{J}$$

$$\text{KE gained} = \text{PE lost}$$
$$\tfrac{1}{2}\,mv^2 = 1\,000\,000\,\text{J} \text{ (see page 57 for the equation for KE)}$$

$$v^2 = \frac{2 \times 1\,000\,000\,\text{J}}{2000\,\text{kg}}$$
$$= 1000\,\text{J/kg}$$
$$v = 31.6\,\text{m/s}$$

2 The KE of a roller coaster car at the bottom of a slope is 1 200 000 J. The mass of the car is 1500 kg and its speed at the top was 0 m/s. How high was the slope? (Use g = 10 N/kg.)

$$\text{PE lost} = \text{KE gained}$$
$$\text{PE lost} = mgh$$
$$1500\,\text{kg} \times 10\,\text{N/kg} \times h = 1\,200\,000\,\text{J}$$
$$h = 80\,\text{m}$$

More about kinetic energy

KE = ½ mv² (see page 57)

If the mass is 1 kg and the speed is 1 m/s
KE = ½ × 1 × 1 × 1 = 0.5 J

Doubling the mass doubles the KE:
KE = ½ × 2 × 1 × 1 = 1 J

Doubling the speed quadruples the KE:
KE = ½ × 1 × 2 × 2 = 4 J

Test yourself

1 Jessica pulls the swing to point A in the diagram. She lets it go without pushing and it swings down through point B and up to C. Which statements (A–D) are true?

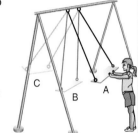

C   B   A

   A The swing has maximum PE at B.
   B The swing has maximum PE at A and C.
   C The swing has maximum KE at B.
   D The swing has maximum KE at A and C.

2 Which has the most PE, a 10 kg weight 6 m above the surface of the Earth or the same weight 6 m above the surface of the Moon?

3 A roller coaster car starts with a speed of zero at the top of a 20 m high slope. The car has a mass of 2000 kg.

   (a) Use the equation PE = mgh and g = 10 N/kg to work out the PE of the car at the top of the slope.
   (b) The car rolls down the slope. What happens to its PE?
   (c) Use the equation KE = ½ mv² to work out the speed of the car at the bottom of the slope.

4 (a) Car A has 90 000 J of KE. How much KE will it have if it travels at double the speed?
   (b) Car B travels at the same speed as car A, and has twice the KE. Why is this?

5 Using g = 10 N/kg, work out:

   (a) the weight of a 60 kg woman
   (b) the mass of a chocolate bar weighing 1 N.

P4a Electrostatic sparks

After revising this item you should:

● be able to explain electron movement and that electrostatic charges can attract and repel and cause electric shocks, and describe some of the dangers and problems they cause.

Electric charge

There are two types of electric charge: positive charge and negative charge.

● Materials that are positively charged have missing electrons.
● Materials that are negatively charged have extra electrons.

Like charges **repel** and unlike charges **attract**.

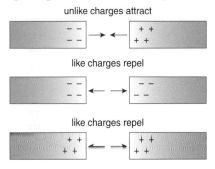

Electrostatic phenomena are caused by the transfer of electrons.

When insulators are rubbed, electrons are rubbed off one material and transferred to the other. This results in effects called electrostatic phenomena or **static electricity**.

Electric shocks

We feel a flow of electrons through our bodies because our nerves detect the flow. We call this an **electric shock**.

Electrostatic shocks are usually small and not harmful. Larger ones can be dangerous to people with heart problems. The flow of charge through the body can stop the heart.

Lightning is a very large electrostatic discharge. It can jump from a cloud to a building. If it flows through a body it is often fatal.

The earth connection

To discharge objects, or stop them becoming charged, we connect them with a thick metal wire to a large metal plate in the ground. This acts as a large reservoir of electrons. We call this an earth connection, and objects that are connected this way are said to be earthed.

Electrons flow so quickly to or from earth that earthed objects do not become charged. If all the metal water pipes in a house are connected into the ground like this they can be used as an earth.

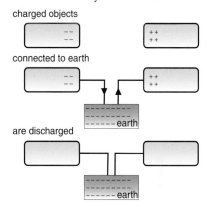

Electric shocks can also occur with electricity from batteries or the mains supply. The mains supply is much more dangerous than batteries or static. The metal cases of electrical appliances must be earthed to prevent electric shocks if there is a fault.

If you stand on an insulating mat you can become electrostatically charged more easily. When you step off the mat the charge will leak away through your shoes. If you wear shoes with insulating soles you will stay charged until you touch something that is earthed.

Dangerous static electricity

When an object is discharged the electrons jump across the gap just before the two objects touch. This is a spark. It can cause an explosion if:

● the atmosphere contains inflammable gases like hydrogen or methane
● there are inflammable vapours like petrol or methanol
● there is a high concentration of oxygen. This includes powders in the air, like flour or custard, which are carbohydrates. They contain lots of oxygen and burn easily. As a dust they can explode.

A nuisance

Small particles of dust and dirt are attracted to charged objects, for example:

- plastic cases   • TV monitors.

Clothing 'clings' to other items of clothing or to the body when it is charged, because it is attracted to oppositely charged or uncharged objects.

Anti-static sprays, liquids and cloths stop the build up of static charge and help reduce these problems.

Exam tip

Remember that electrostatics is about the transfer of (negatively charged) electrons. Think of the earth connection as a huge reservoir of electrons.

Test yourself

1 When they are rubbed, what happens:
   - (a) to some materials to make them positively charged
   - (b) to other materials to make them negatively charged?

2 A polythene rod is rubbed with a duster and hung up on a piece of thread.
   - (a) What happens when a second rubbed polythene rod is brought close to it?
   - (b) When a perspex rod is rubbed and brought close to it, the polythene is attracted to the perspex. What does this tell you about the two materials?

3 Explain why is there a risk of explosion in a flour mill.

4 Explain why a petrol tanker must be earthed before it is unloaded.

5 (a) Why does dust stick to television monitors?
   (b) How can this problem be reduced?

P4b Uses of electrostatics

After revising this item you should:

- be able to explain how electrostatic charge can be used in defibrillators, electrostatic precipitators and to improve paint spraying.

Defibrillators

A **defibrillator** is used to start the heart when it has stopped. It works because the flow of electric charge makes muscles contract.

1 Paddles are placed on the patients chest – they must make a good electrical contact.

2 Everyone including the operator must 'stand clear' so they don't get an electric shock.

3 The paddles are charged.

4 The charge is passed through the plates to make the heart contract.

How science works

All the examples in this section are applications of electrostatic charge, designed for our benefit. Some have a risk of electrostatic shock, but, with care, we have designed safe appliances and safe working practices.

Electrostatic dust precipitators

Electrostatic dust precipitators remove smoke particles from chimneys before they are carried out by the hot air and cause pollution. The precipitators make use of electrostatic charge to attract the smoke particles or dust.

1 Metal plates or grids are put in the chimneys.

2 They are charged by connecting them to a high potential difference (pd) or voltage.

3 The dust particles are attracted to the charged plates or grids.

4 They clump together on the plates to form larger particles.

5 When they are heavy enough, the dust particles fall back down the chimney into containers.

Depending on the design, dust can be:

- positively charged and attracted to negatively charged plates, or
- negatively charged and attracted to positively charged plates.

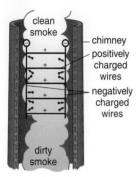

✎ charged dust particles attracted to plates

Paint spraying

Paint spraying can also make use of static electricity.

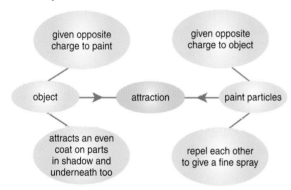

Test yourself

1 A defibrillator is used to restart a heart which has stopped beating.

   (a) Why is the patient's shirt undone and the paddles placed directly on the skin?

   (b) Why does the operator tell everyone to stand clear?

   (c) What effect does the charge have on the heart to make it start beating?

2 An electrostatic precipitator is installed in a chimney. The smoke particles pick up negative charge as they pass a negatively charged grid.

   (a) Why do the smoke particles travel up the chimney?

   (b) Name the particles that make the smoke particles negatively charged.

3 Smoke particles are attracted to charged plates in an electrostatic precipitator. They form a thick layer which falls off when the plates are hit with hammers.

   (a) What is the charge on the plates?

   (b) Why does the smoke layer fall down and not go up the chimney?

4 A paint spraying system uses opposite charges on the paint particles and the car body.

   (a) Explain what effect the electric charges have when paint is sprayed towards the car.

   (b) Explain why less paint is wasted using this system.

   (c) Give another benefit of the system.

5 Which of these statements (A–F) are true?

   A A defibrillator uses electric charge to make the heart contract.

   B A defibrillator could stop the heart if it is beating already.

   C An electrostatic paint sprayer uses the same charge on the paint and the object to be painted.

   D An electrostatic precipitator attracts smoke particles out of the top of a chimney.

   E In an electrostatic precipitator the smoke particles are given a charge.

   F In an electrostatic precipitator the charge on the plates is reversed to make the smoke particles fall off

P4c Safe electric circuits

After revising this item you should:

- be able to explain how an electric circuit works, describe how a variable resistor can change the current in a circuit, calculate resistance and explain how fuses and circuit breakers make circuits safer.

Electric circuits

A flow of electric charge in a **circuit** is called a current. We can use variable resistors to change the current in a circuit.

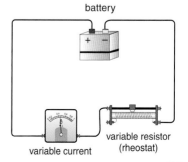

variable current

variable resistor (rheostat)

The **resistance** of a **variable resistor**, or **rheostat**, can be:

- increased by moving the slider to make the wire longer
- decreased by moving the slider to make the wire shorter.

When the resistance increases the current decreases.

How science works

Variable resistors are found inside joystick controls used for all kinds of things, from computer games to wheelchairs.

As you move the joystick back and forth you change the resistance of one variable resistor. For the side-to-side movement there is a second variable resistor.

Changing the resistance changes the current, so the position of the stick is translated into an electrical signal for the computer.

Current, potential difference and resistance

Current:

- passes **through** wires or components
- is measured in amperes or amps (A) using an ammeter.

Voltage or **potential difference** (pd):

- is set up **across** a wire or a component – between the two ends
- is measured in volts (V) using a voltmeter.

Exam tip

You must know these electric circuit symbols for the exam.

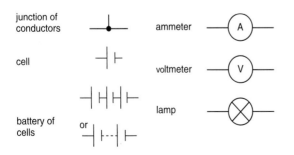

junction of conductors		ammeter	A
cell		voltmeter	V
battery of cells	or	lamp	

The circuit diagram shows a circuit used for two experiments.

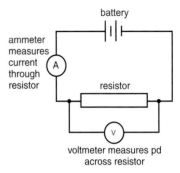

ammeter measures current through resistor

voltmeter measures pd across resistor

The first experiment uses the same resistor and different batteries.

- Increasing the pd across the resistor increases the current through it.
- Decreasing the pd across the resistor decreases the current through it.

Resistance:

The second experiment uses the same battery and different resistors.

When you have a fixed pd (e.g. a 9 V battery):

- increasing the resistance decreases the current
- decreasing the resistance increases the current.

To find resistance you use the formula:

$$\text{resistance (ohms)} = \frac{\text{voltage (V)}}{\text{current (A)}}$$

For example:

1   A 9 volt battery is connected to a resistor and the current is 0.9 amps. What is the resistance?

$$\text{resistance} = \frac{9\,\text{V}}{0.9\,\text{A}}$$
$$= 10 \text{ ohms}$$

2   A 100 ohm resistor is connected to the 240 V mains electricity supply. What is the current?

$$\text{current} = \frac{\text{voltage}}{\text{resistance}}$$
$$= \frac{240\,\text{V}}{100 \text{ ohms}}$$
$$= 2.4\,\text{A}$$

voltage

resistance   current
(If you need a reminder of how to use the triangle, see P3a Speed on page 51.)

Exam tip

Remember: 'current **through**' and 'voltage **across**'.

Mains wiring

Wire	Colour	Purpose
live wire	brown	the high voltage connection
neutral wire	blue	second wire to complete the circuit
earth wire	yellow and green	safety wire to stop the appliance becoming live

A conductor is live when it is connected to the electricity supply by the live or neutral wire. If you touch it you get an electric shock that could be fatal.

Conductors, like the metal cases of appliances, cannot become live if they are connected to the earth wire.

Fuses and circuit breakers

A **fuse** is a thin piece of wire. It is a weak link in the circuit.

If the current gets too large, the fuse:

- will melt
- break the circuit and prevents the flow of current.

This prevents the flex overheating and causing fire which prevents further damage to the appliance.

Fuses will not stop you getting an electric shock – they take too long to melt. After it has melted the fuse must be replaced.

- A 2 amp fuse melts when a current of 2 amps flows through it.
- A 13 amp fuse melts when 13 amps flows through it.

You should fit the lowest fuse that will carry the normal operating current.

Circuit breakers are switches that switch the current off when it gets too high. They can be switched on again once the fault is corrected.

A residual current device (RCD) is a circuit breaker that switches off very quickly. It will protect you from receiving an electric shock.

Electric shocks, the fuse and the earth wire

Touching a live appliance could result in a fatal electric shock.

The fuse and the earth wire can be used together to prevent the metal casing of an electric appliance becoming live.

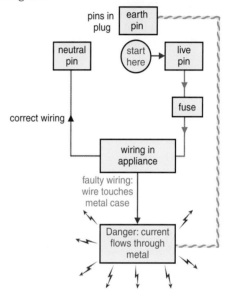

Use the diagram to help you follow what happens.

Circuit	Starts at	Route
correct	live pin of the plug	through the fuse ↓ through the appliance ↓ back to the neutral pin
faulty	live pin of the plug	through the fuse ↓ through the appliance ↓ through the faulty connection to the metal case ↓ through the metal case ↓ through the earth wire to the earth. This will be such a huge current that it will melt the fuse and break the faulty circuit, stopping the current.

Double insulated appliances

Double insulated appliances do not need earthing because the case of the appliance is not a conductor, so it cannot become live.

1. (a) Vicky is changing the pd across a resistor, and measuring the current through it. Describe what happens to the current when she decreases the pd.
   (b) She keeps the pd constant and changes the resistor to one with higher resistance. What happens to the current?

2. The current in a light bulb is 0.4 A when it is connected to the 240 V mains supply. Work out the resistance of the light bulb.

3. (a) The current through a 2000 ohm resistor is 0.12 amps. What is the pd across the resistor?
   (b) The pd across a 300 ohm resistor is 9 volts. What is the current through it?

4. (a) How does a fuse protect the wires in an appliance from overheating?
   (b) Choose the correct fuse, either 3 amp or 13 amp, for each appliance:
      (i) A kettle with normal current 11 amps.
      (ii) A hairdryer with normal current 4 amps.
      (iii) A light bulb with normal current 0.4 amps.

5. (a) What is the advantage of using a circuit breaker instead of a fuse?
   (b) What is meant by a 'double insulated' appliance?
   (c) Why is the earth wire connected to the case of a metal appliance?

P4d Ultrasound & P4e Treatment

- be able to describe features of longitudinal and transverse waves, recall that ultrasound is a longitudinal wave, compare X-rays and gamma rays and describe medical applications of ultrasound, beta radiation, gamma rays and X-rays.

Longitudinal waves

A longitudinal wave can be made to travel along a slinky spring. In a longitudinal wave the vibrations are back and forth, parallel to the direction of travel.

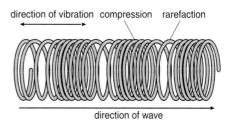

direction of vibration   compression   rarefaction

direction of wave

- **Compression** – where the particles are closest together (in the spring the coils are bunched together).
- **Rarefaction** – where the particles are furthest apart (in the spring the coils are spread out).
- Amplitude – the maximum distance a particle moves from its normal position (in the spring the maximum distance of a coil from where it would be if no wave disturbed it).
- Wavelength – the distance before the wave repeats (e.g. between two compressions or between two rarefactions).
- Frequency – the number of waves passing a point in one second (e.g. the number of compressions passing a point in one second).

The lines in this diagram represent layers of air particles. If there was no wave they would be evenly spaced.

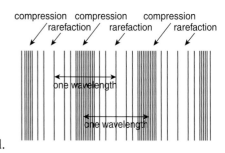

compression compression   compression
rarefaction / rarefaction / rarefaction

one wavelength

one wavelength

The second type of wave is the transverse wave.

In a transverse wave the particles vibrate at right angles to the direction the wave is travelling.

Both longitudinal and transverse waves carry energy, but not material. The particles vibrate, moving:
- up and down
- back and forward
- side to side

but the particles do not get carried along with the wave.

Ultrasound

Ultrasound is a longitudinal wave.

Ultrasound waves are sound waves with a frequency that is higher than the **upper threshold of human hearing**.

Ultrasound in medicine

body scans	the ultrasound beam is sent into the body. Each time it crosses a boundary between different tissues some is reflected. These reflections from different layers are built up into a picture by a computer.
	Ultrasound is reflected from soft tissues so it can detect things that X-rays cannot. It does not damage living cells like X-rays so it is safer.
breaking down stones	the vibrations caused by ultrasound waves can break down accumulations, e.g. kidney stones.

Nuclear radiation and X-rays

Beta radiation and **gamma rays** are used in nuclear medicine because they can pass through the skin. (Alpha radiation cannot.)

X-rays are easier to control than gamma rays.

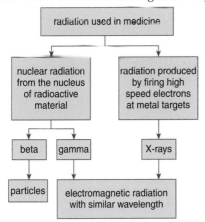

Cancer treatment

Alpha and beta radiation, and gamma and X-rays, can damage or kill living cells. There is always a risk in using them, but they can be beneficial.

Gamma rays are used to treat cancer:

- Gamma rays are focused on the tumour.
- A wide beam is used. This is rotated round the patient, keeping the tumour at the centre.
- The tumour receives a concentrated dose of gamma rays. The non-cancerous tissue gets a weak dose, which limits the damage

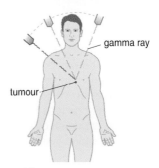

Treating a tumour with gamma rays.

Medical tracers

Radioactive medical **tracers** are materials that emit beta radiation or gamma rays.

A tracer is ingested by the patient. (The tracer could be drunk, eaten, injected or even breathed in as a gas.)

The doctors wait for the tracer to spread through the body. Different tracers are used for different parts of the body. Doctors choose a tracer that, once inside the body, is carried to the part they want to investigate.

The beta radiation (or gamma rays) pass out of the body. Doctors use a radiation detector to record them, e.g. a gamma camera.

How science works

When X-rays and radioactive materials were first discovered, all kinds of claims were made about the health benefits. There were some strange health treatments that exposed people to high doses. Some people suffered cell damage and cancer and some died.

Gradually evidence built up that this type of radiation was dangerous and safety precautions were introduced. In the 1950s all pregnant women were X-rayed. Today only essential X-rays are done.

Test yourself

1 (a) Describe how the particles move:
   (i) in a transverse wave
   (ii) in a longitudinal wave.
   (b) Describe what happens to the particles if the amplitude of the transverse wave increases.
   (c) What is meant by the wavelength of a longitudinal wave?

2 Explain how an ultrasound scan of a fetus is taken.

3 Describe one way that gamma rays are similar to X-rays and one way that they are different.

4 Which of these statements (A–G) are true?

   A   Gamma rays are used to treat cancer.
   B   Beta radiation does not damage living cells.
   C   X-rays can be used as tracers.
   D   Tracers are radioactive materials that emit beta radiation or gamma rays.
   E   Some tracers are drunk by the patient.
   F   A tracer is a beam of gamma rays fired at a patient.
   G   A gamma camera is used outside the patient to detect gamma rays emitted by the tracer inside the patient.

5 (a)   Describe how the damage to a patient's healthy cells is kept to a minimum when a tumour is treated with gamma rays.
    (b)   Describe how the risk to the radiographer is kept to a minimum.

P4f What is radioactivity?

After revising this item you should:

●   be able to explain what is meant by radioactive half-life and describe what happens to a nucleus when an alpha particle or a beta particle is emitted.

Radioactive materials

Radioactive substances contain radioactive nuclei that **decay** naturally and emit nuclear radiation.

The nuclear radiation can be:

● alpha   ● beta   ● gamma

Half-life

Half-life is the average time for half of a sample of radioactive nuclei to decay.

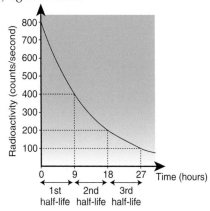

The following diagram shows a sample of radioactive nuclei with a half-life of 6 hours.

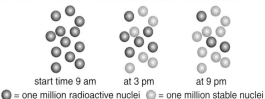

start time 9 am   at 3 pm   at 9 pm
● = one million radioactive nuclei   ● = one million stable nuclei

After one half-life, half of the original nuclei are left. After two half-lives, one quarter of the original nuclei are left.

For example:

A radioactive sample has a half-life of 5 hours. How long will it take for the count rate to drop from 60 counts per minute to 15 counts per minute?

$$60 \times \tfrac{1}{2} = 30, \; 30 \times \tfrac{1}{2} = 15$$

so it will take 2 half-lives = 2 × 5 hours
                          = 10 hours.

Radioactive decay is often plotted as a graph of radioactivity (the number of decays emitted per second) against time.

In the diagram the activity halves from 800 to 400 in 9 hours, so the half-life is 9 hours.

Notice that it also takes 9 hours to drop from 400 to 200.

To drop from 800 to 100 is three half-lives (one half of one half of one half = one eighth).

Alpha radiation

An **alpha particle** (also called **alpha radiation**) is:

● made up of two protons and two neutrons
● the same as a fast moving helium nucleus.

Alpha decay

An alpha particle is written $_2^4\alpha$.

This means:

- 2 protons: atomic number = 2
- 2 protons and 2 neutrons: mass number = 4.

For example, the diagram on the right shows what happens when radon decays by emitting an alpha particle.

$$_{86}^{219}\text{Rn} \longrightarrow {}_{84}^{215}\text{Po} + {}_2^4\alpha$$

The new nucleus is polonium. It has two less protons and two less neutrons than radon.

unstable nucleus

↓

loses alpha particle:
2 protons +
2 neutrons

↓

new element:
mass number down 4
atomic number down 2

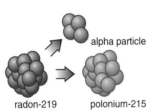

alpha particle

radon-219   polonium-215

Beta radiation

A **beta particle** (also called beta radiation) is:

- a very fast moving electron
- thrown out of the decaying nucleus.

The nucleus has no electrons – think of it as one neutron changing into a proton and an electron. The electron leaves as a beta particle and the proton stays in the nucleus.

unstable nucleus

↓

loses beta particle:
negative charge
negligible mass

↓

new element:
mass number unchanged
atomic number up 1

Beta decay

The new element has one more proton and one less neutron.

A beta particle is written $_{-1}^{0}\beta$.

For example, the diagram on the right shows what happens when carbon decays by beta radiation to form nitrogen.

$$_6^{14}\text{C} \longrightarrow {}_7^{14}\text{N} + {}_{-1}^{0}\beta$$

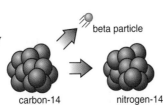

beta particle

carbon-14   nitrogen-14

Exam tip

Remember: alpha particles and beta particles are thrown out of decaying nuclei. Alpha particles are not helium atoms and beta particles are not electrons from the electron shell of an atom.

Test yourself

1 What is:
- (a) radioactive half-life
- (b) an alpha particle
- (c) a beta particle?

2 Technetium-99 (Tc-99) has a half-life of 6 hours.
- (a) If there are 128 million atoms in a sample, how many are left after 7 half-lives?
- (b) How long does it take for the activity of a Tc-99 source to fall from 40 counts per minute to 10 counts per minute?
- (c) If a patient is injected with a dose of Tc-99, what fraction is left after 24 hours?

3 (a) Use this graph to complete the table below.

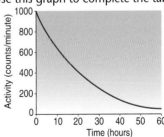

Activity (counts/min)	Time (hours)
1000	
	10
500	
	25

(b) Use the table to decide the half-life of the source.

4 Uranium-238 decays by alpha emission to thorium.

(a) What happens to the protons and neutrons in the nucleus when an alpha particle is emitted?

(b) Copy and complete this equation for the decay.

$$^{238}_{92}U \longrightarrow ^{?}_{?}\alpha + ^{?}_{?}Th$$

5 Boron-12 decays by beta emission to carbon.

(a) What happens to the protons and neutrons in a nucleus when a beta particle is emitted?

(b) Copy and complete this equation for the decay.

$$^{12}_{5}B \longrightarrow ^{?}_{?}\beta + ^{?}_{?}C$$

P4g Uses of radioisotopes & P4h Fission

After revising these items you should:

● be able to explain where background radiation comes from and describe and explain some uses of radioactivity, including dating and nuclear reactors.

Background radiation

Background radiation is in the environment all the time. It is caused by radioactive substances and varies from place to place.

The diagram shows the different origins of background radiation.

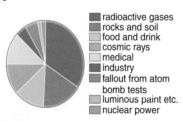

- radioactive gases
- rocks and soil
- food and drink
- cosmic rays
- medical
- industry
- fallout from atom bomb tests
- luminous paint etc.
- nuclear power

How science works

The nuclear industry is regulated and workers must have special training because of the risk to living cells from radiation.

Industrial use of tracers

A tracer can be used to detect a leak or a blockage in a pipe.

- The tracer is added to the fluid in the pipe.
- A gamma source is used so it can penetrate to the surface.

The diagram shows how the **gamma radiation** from the tracer shows where the leak is. Radiation is detected above X and Y, but is reduced, or not detected, at Z.

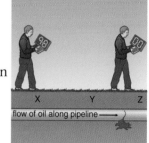

flow of oil along pipeline

Smoke detectors

Alpha sources are used in **smoke detectors**.

- Alpha particles from the source ionise atoms in the air (into electrons and positive ions) so that the air can conduct electricity.
- A small current flows and a sensor detects it.
- If smoke blocks the path of the positive ions and electrons, there is no current and the alarm sounds.

Radioactive dating

Rocks contain radioactive isotopes of uranium. The older the rock, the more of the isotope will have decayed to an isotope of lead. We can use the ratio of uranium to lead to date the rock.

Carbon dating

The amount of carbon-14 in the air has not changed for thousands of years.

The diagram shows how **carbon dating** is used to find the age of a once-living thing.

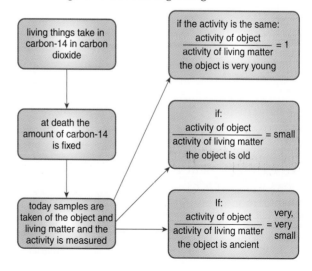

living things take in carbon-14 in carbon dioxide

at death the amount of carbon-14 is fixed

today samples are taken of the object and living matter and the activity is measured

if the activity is the same:
$$\frac{\text{activity of object}}{\text{activity of living matter}} = 1$$
the object is very young

if:
$$\frac{\text{activity of object}}{\text{activity of living matter}} = \text{small}$$
the object is old

If:
$$\frac{\text{activity of object}}{\text{activity of living matter}} = \text{very, very small}$$
the object is ancient

Nuclear power

Electricity is generated in a nuclear power station.

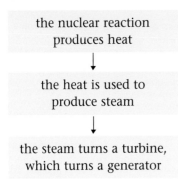

the nuclear reaction produces heat

↓

the heat is used to produce steam

↓

the steam turns a turbine, which turns a generator

Nuclear fission

In the process of **nuclear fission**:

1 A uranium nucleus is hit by a neutron.
2 It absorbs the neutron and becomes unstable.
3 The unstable nucleus splits in two.
4 Energy is given out – this energy is harnessed in a nuclear reactor.
5 The two smaller nuclei produced are radioactive waste.

As each uranium nucleus splits, more than one neutron is given out. These neutrons can cause other uranium atoms to split and lead to a **chain reaction**.

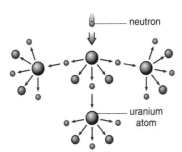

neutron

uranium atom

A nuclear bomb is a chain reaction that has run out of control.

Controlling nuclear reactions

A nuclear reactor has control rods made of a material that absorbs neutrons. Scientists lower the rods into the reactor to absorb some of the neutrons.

They allow just enough neutrons to remain to keep the process operating.

Useful isotopes and radioactive waste

When materials are placed in a nuclear reactor some of the nuclei absorb extra neutrons. This makes them radioactive.

Test yourself

1 Look at the diagram on page 72 showing sources of background radiation.

   (a) Estimate the fraction of background radiation from:
      (i) cosmic rays
      (ii) radioactive gases.
   (b) Explain why background is not the same everywhere.

2 (a) Which isotope is used to date objects that were once living?
   (b) How does the isotope get into:
      (i) living plants
      (ii) living animals.
   (c) Explain how the age of the object is worked out.
   (d) What has to remain constant for this method to work?

3 A sample of living bone has an activity of 60 counts per minute. Using the half-life of carbon-14 (= 5500 years) work out the age of these samples:

Sample	Activity (counts per minute)
X	30
Y	15
Z	60

4 Explain the following terms:

   (a) nuclear fission (b) chain reaction
   (c) nuclear reactor (d) control rods.

5 (a) Name a fuel used in a nuclear reactor.
   (b) What is needed to start the fission reaction?
   (c) Why does the reaction keep going?
   (d) How do scientists stop it going out of control?

Exam-style questions

1 (a) Use examples to explain the difference between unicellular and multicellular organisms.

....

....[2]

(b) Explain the advantages of being multicellular.

....

....

....[3]

(c) Complete the diagrams by writing the number of chromosomes in the circles. [2]

mitosis   meiosis

parent (46)   (46)
cell

offspring

(d) During growth, cells and organisms enlarge in size. How is plant cell growth different to animal cell growth?

....

....

....[3]

2 (a) In a glasshouse the tomato plant leaves start turning yellow.

(i) Which two mineral elements are missing?

....

....[2]

(ii) How could the grower make the leaves green again?

....[1]

(b) There are more minerals in the root of a plant than in the soil, yet minerals are taken up from the soil. Explain how this can occur.

....

....[2]

(c) When the tomatoes have been harvested, the grower wants to recycle the nutrients still in the green parts of the plant. Suggest how she could do this.

....[1]

(d) The tomatoes are sold and some go to the canning factory. Explain how canning the tomatoes preserves them for longer than keeping them in a refrigerator.

....

....

....[3]

3 (a) Sodium is a metal in Group 1 and iron is a transition element.
State **one** property of a compound of a transition element that is not shown by a Group 1 metal compound.

....[1]

(b) Sodium compounds can be identified using a flame test. Describe how to carry out a flame test.

....

....

....[3]

(c) The table below shows some properties of some Group 1 metals.

Element	Boiling point (°C)	Reaction with oxygen
sodium	883	steadily
potassium	760	rapidly
rubidium	698	
caesium		explosively

(i) Predict the boiling point of caesium.

....[1]

(ii) Predict how rubidium will react with oxygen.

....[1]

(d) Iron has a high melting point. Use ideas about the bonding in iron to explain why this is.

....

....

....[3]

(e) Iron(II) carbonate, $FeCO_3$, decomposes when heated. Write a balanced symbol equation for this reaction.

....[1]

4 (a) Diamond and graphite are forms of carbon. What name is given to different forms of the same element?

....[1]

(b) What property of graphite makes it useful as a lubricant?

....[1]

(c) Explain why graphite conducts electricity.

....[1]

(d) Nanotubes are also a form of carbon. Nanotubes can be used in catalysis.
Explain how and why nanotubes are used in catalysis.

....

....[2]

(e) In a blast furnace, carbon is heated with iron(III) oxide to form iron and carbon monoxide.

$$Fe_2O_3 + 3CO \longrightarrow 2Fe + 3CO_2$$

Calculate the mass of iron formed when 320 tonnes of iron(III) oxide react completely. (O = 16, Fe = 56)

....

....

....

....

....[3]

(f) Most dry-cleaning fluids are carbon-based organic molecules. Explain in terms of intermolecular forces how dry-cleaning fluids remove the greasy dirt from clothes.

....

....

....[2]

5 At a skydiving club, Sonia is flying an aircraft with a take-off speed of 32 m/s.
The aircraft accelerates from 0 to 32 m/s in 8 s.

(a) Calculate the acceleration of the aircraft.

....

....

....[2]

(b) In the air, the aircraft accelerates at $2.5 \, m/s^2$ from a speed of 32 m/s to its cruising speed of 82 m/s. Calculate the time to reach cruising speed.

....

....

....[2]

(c) The aircraft has a mass of 3800 kg. Calculate the kinetic energy it has at cruising speed.

....

....

....[2]

Jim begins his skydive from the aircraft.

(d) Label the two forces on Jim as he starts falling. [2]

(e) After a few seconds Jim reaches a steady speed. Why does he reach a steady speed?

....[1]

6 In hospitals, ultrasound is used for scanning parts of the body.

(a) Give **two** reasons why ultrasound is used, and not X-rays, to scan the fetus in the womb.

....

....[2]

(b) How is ultrasound different to normal sound?

....

....[2]

(c) Ultrasound is a longitudinal wave. This diagram shows a longitudinal wave in a spring.

direction of vibration

direction of wave

(i) Complete the **three** labels on the diagram. [3]

(ii) Describe how the air particles move when a longitudinal ultrasound wave travels through the air.

....

....[2]

Answers to exam-style questions

1 (a) Amoeba is a unicellular organism made of one cell; Humans are multicellular organisms which means made of many cells [2]

(b) Any **three** from: Allows the organism to be larger; Allows for cell differentiation; Allows the organism to be more complex; A single cell has a smaller surface area to volume ratio, reducing movement of materials in and out [3]

(c) Mitosis – all 46; Meiosis – all 23 [2]

(d) Plant cell division is restricted to shoot and root tips; Plant cells retain the ability to differentiate; Cell enlargement is the main method plants use to increase in height [3]

2 (a) (i) Nitrate; Magnesium [2]

(ii) Add fertiliser [1]

(b) By active uptake; Which uses energy [2]

(c) Make compost with them [1]

(d) Any **three** from: Canning kills bacteria in or on the tomatoes; Bacteria decays food; Canning stops more bacteria from entering; Refrigerator is cold and slows down bacterial growth but does not stop it [3]

3 (a) Transition element compounds are coloured / are catalysts [1]

(b) Moisten a nichrome / platinum wire; Dip the wire into the solid compound; Put the compound on the wire at the edge of a blue Bunsen flame [3]

(c) (i) Values between 620°C and 680°C (actual value is 669°C) [1]

(ii) Very rapidly / indication of more rapidly than potassium but less rapidly than caesium [1]

(d) Metallic bonding due to metal cations / positive ions in sea of electrons / delocalised electrons; Strong forces of attraction between the cations and electrons; Takes a lot of energy to break these strong forces [3]

(e) $FeCO_3 \longrightarrow FeO + CO_2$ [1]

4 (a) Allotrope(s) [1]

(b) Slippery(ness) [1]

(c) Delocalised electrons can move (not electrons can move) [1]

(d) Small groups of catalyst atoms attached to outside of nanotubes; Provide a large surface area for catalysis [2]

(e) RMM of $Fe_2O_3 = (56 \times 2) + (16 \times 3) = 160$; 160 tonnes of Fe_2O_3 will give $56 \times 2 = 112$ tonnes of Fe; 320 tonnes of Fe_2O_3 gives 224 tonnes of Fe (apply transferred error) [3]

(f) Intermolecular forces of attraction between grease molecules and dry-cleaning fluid molecules; Allows grease molecules to dissolve in dry-cleaning fluid [2]

5 (a) Acceleration = change in velocity/time (or a = v/t) = 32/8; $4 m/s^2$ [2]

(b) Time = change in velocity/acceleration (or t = v/a) = 50/2.5; 20 s [2]

(c) $0.5 \times 3800 \times (82)^2$; 12 800 000 / 12 775 600 J [2]

(d) Upwards force: drag; Downwards force: weight [2]

(e) Drag = weight / drag increases [1]

6 (a) Can image soft tissues; Does not damage soft tissue / X-rays do damage soft tissue [2]

(b) Higher frequency; Above threshold of human hearing [2]

(c) (i) Left to right: Wavelength; Compression; Rarefaction [3]

(ii) Back and forth / oscillate; In / parallel to direction of travel [2]

Index of key words